SOCIETY FOR NEW TESTAMENT STUDIES

MONOGRAPH SERIES

General Editor: Matthew Black, D.D., F.B.A.
Associate Editor: R. McL. Wilson

32

ON THE INDEPENDENCE OF
MATTHEW AND MARK

On the independence of Matthew and Mark

JOHN M. RIST

Professor of Classics and Philosophy, University of Toronto

CAMBRIDGE UNIVERSITY PRESS

CAMBRIDGE

LONDON · NEW YORK · MELBOURNE

Published by the Syndics of the Cambridge University Press
The Pitt Building, Trumpington Street, Cambridge CB2 1RP
Bentley House, 200 Euston Road, London NW1 2DB
32 East 57th Street, New York NY10022, USA
296 Beaconsfield Parade, Middle Park, Melbourne 3206, Australia

First published 1978

Printed in Great Britain at
the University Press, Cambridge

Library of Congress Cataloguing in Publication Data
Rist, John M.
On the independence of Matthew and Mark.
(Monograph series - Society for New Testament Studies; 32)
Includes bibliographical references and index.
1. Bible. N.T. Matthew - Relation to Mark.
2. Bible. N.T. Mark - Relation to Matthew
I. Title. II. Series: Studorium Novi Testamenti Societas. Monograph series; 32.
BS25 75. 2. R58 226′ .2′06 76-40840
ISBN 0 521 21476 9

CONTENTS

AUTHOR'S NOTE

Some of the conclusions of this monograph were presented to the Oriental Club of Toronto; I should like to thank the members of the Club for their patience and comments. After being bored by Q in a popularized version in my schooldays, my interest in the Synoptics was re-aroused by George Goold, whose critical comments on the manuscript were most helpful even when wrong. Frank Beare and Timothy Barnes also read an earlier draft and tolerated more of it than I had expected. I discussed the major thesis and many of the details with Anna Rist. Much of what is here is hers; I cannot now disentangle what was hers and what was mine.

Pian Rocchetto, Semproniano, 1976   John Rist

1

PROBLEMS AND ASSUMPTIONS

Far too much has already been written on the Synoptic Problem. General studies and detailed work on small portions of the question have accumulated year after year. At this stage the only justification for another monograph is either a contribution of overlooked or unrealized facts, or an examination of axioms which, through long and uncritical acceptance, have stood in the way of progress and have generated unnecessary paradoxes. A recent provocative and illuminating book[1] has shown us how it was necessary in the latter part of the nineteenth century and the early part of the twentieth for many theologians and scripture scholars to believe that Mark was the first of the Synoptic Gospels. For Mark, they thought, contained less legendary material and less miraculous happenings; and if they were to remain Christians in a rational age, this was a Gospel in which they could more readily place their attenuated faith. Such details as the Infancy Narratives and the Resurrection Appearances must represent a mythologizing, theologizing or paganizing of the original primitive tradition.

The classical form of the orthodox doctrine that Mark is the earliest of the Synoptics and that Matthew and Luke have combined Mark with a second document, given the shorthand title Q (German *Quelle*), was provided by B. H. Streeter in his magisterial book *The Four Gospels*.[2] The ground, of course, had been diligently tilled before Streeter, and in the course of the tilling many valuable finds came to light, but the really impressive result of Streeter's work was that, with few exceptions, largely of the Roman persuasion, scholars were prepared to accept the so-called Two-Document theory - many indeed have continued to do so - even though the arguments on which the hypothesis was *originally* based have been found inadequate.[3] We are confronted here with a not unfamiliar syndrome in scholarship: my result must be right; if my reasons for subscribing to it are demonstrably false, I must hunt up some more. As an example of this approach we may cite the comment of G. M. Styler: 'It seems that, however insecure the arguments used in the past, the reasons for accepting the priority of Mark

are in fact strong.'[4]   And we are now frequently told that great advances
have been made in our understanding of the Synoptics by the method of
Redaktionsgeschichte, which often seems to involve considering how Mark
and Luke have reworked the *theology* of Mark; enquiries of this kind necessarily imply the use of Markan priority as a working hypothesis.[5]   So pres-
tigious has this approach become that even a number of Roman Catholic
scholars, perhaps motivated in part by a misguided ecumenism, have found
that their interest in *Redaktionsgeschichte* has led them towards an un-
traditional acceptance of the Two-Document theory.[6]

An uncritical acceptance of the axioms and presuppositions of the
Markan priorists is not the only, or indeed the most basic, methodological
problem with which we are faced. For such has been the authority of
Streeter and the tradition of which his work was the culmination, that even
the dissidents have been almost universally tempted to see the problem in
the terms that have been authorized. Those scholars who have wanted to
argue the Augustinian position that Matthew (or an Aramaic Matthew) is
the earliest Gospel,[7] and that Mark depends on Matthew, have accepted the
orthodox view that the problem is one of direct literary dependence. Thus
Butler argued that Peter, the primary source of Mark, used a Greek Matthew
(a 'complete and authentic translation' of the original Aramaic Matthew) as
his aide-memoire,[8] while Vaganay wanted us to believe that Mark (Peter?)
had two sources, a Greek Matthew (derived from an Aramaic Matthew) and
a Sayings Source (Sg), also in Greek.[9]   Farmer too, though bold enough to
revert to the untenable thesis of Griesbach that Mark is some sort of summary based on Matthew and Luke, still operates within the bounds of literary source criticism;[10] as most recently does one of his disciples, Dungan,
who, while deploring the logic of Streeter in deducing, from the facts that
Matthew reproduced 90% of the subject matter of Mark in largely identical
language and that Luke reproduces a bit more than half of Mark, the conclusion that Mark is therefore *prior* to Matthew and Luke, still concludes
no more than that 'all Streeter's statement proves is that Mark is in some
sort of literary relation with Matthew and Luke'.[11]

There are, of course, a number of facts about Matthew, Mark and Luke
which might seem to justify such proceedings. They must therefore be
summarized at the outset.[12]   About eleven twelfths of Mark's subject-
matter appears in Matthew and over half of it appears in Luke. In passages
where the same incidents are narrated in all three Gospels, that is, in the so-
called Triple Tradition, many of Mark's actual Greek words appear in
Matthew, or Luke, or both; 51% of Mark's words appear in Matthew. Furthermore, Matthew and Luke generally agree with Mark's order in presenting
their pericopae, and where one of them diverges in this ordering (and Luke

diverges very rarely), the other normally follows Mark's order. In fact not only do Matthew and Luke rarely agree against Mark in wording and in the syntax of their sentences, they almost never agree against Mark in the matter of arrangement.[13] Again, it was said, after the account of the Temptation, Matthew and Luke never agree in inserting a particular piece of Q material into the same context in Mark. Finally, so it was claimed, it must be the case that when we are dealing with literary relationships, the most primitive writing is necessarily the oldest. Markan priorists then claimed to show that Mark is clearly more primitive, while supporters of Matthew countered by bringing up the argument that since many Matthaean passages are the more primitive, Matthew must therefore be the source of the less primitive version of the same events in Mark, and, in some cases perhaps, in Luke.[14]

As our problem was traditionally posed, either Mark, with Matthew and various other material at his disposal, sits down to write a new Gospel, or Matthew, already in possession of Mark and Q, begins his work of assimilation.[15] Let us look at this more closely. In a community where a copy of Matthew is already available, why should someone write another Gospel like our Mark? It is shorter than Matthew, omits a great deal of Matthew, most obviously the Infancy Narrative, the Sermon on the Mount and the Resurrection Appearances. What purpose would it serve? Perhaps purposes can be excogitated. Farmer, as we noted, thought of a 'mixed' community in Alexandria or Rome for whom a summary of Matthew and Luke would be an indication of a single common tradition. But if so, how do we explain omitting the Lord's Prayer, the Beatitudes and the Nativity?[16] In fact, the most obvious motive for a new production would be that the author (for 'heretical' reasons) wished to *suppress* some of the Matthaean material. According to Irenaeus and Epiphanius, we have recently been reminded, Marcion did in fact produce a 'version' of Luke stripped of the Infancy Narratives and much of Jesus' teaching, while Irenaeus tells us that some of the Docetists preferred Mark because it seemed to support their own theological idiosyncracies better.[17]So the theoretical possibility exists that Mark could have been produced as a deliberate re-writing of Matthew or Luke. But in fact there is no evidence and no tradition at all that this was what happened. There is no significant association of Mark's Gospel with those wishing to suppress elements of Matthew or Luke. Mark's Gospel is not only assumed to be thoroughly orthodox; it was also, in fact, comparatively neglected in antiquity. So if its author intended it to replace Matthew and Luke, the least that can be said is that he totally misjudged his audience. So far as we can tell, it was Matthew's Gospel which enjoyed the greatest vogue among the Synoptics, and the problem still remains with us that, heresy aside, it is hard to explain the composition of

Mark in any Christian community if Matthew, or indeed any other substantive and authoritative literary document, was already available in that community. Of course, if the community which generated Mark did not possess Matthew, then there is an obvious need of a written text whether Matthew was in fact in existence or not. Butler, it may be noted, was perhaps aware of difficulties about the appearance of Mark in a 'Matthaean' community when he claimed that Mark was 'Peter's counter-signature to the witness of his fellow-apostle in Matthew', and if, as Butler supposes, there are reasons why the claim that Mark depends on Matthew cannot be denied, perhaps we should accept this as the best explanation of facts available in the circumstances. But there are reasons to think that Butler's case is not as strong as he believes.

If we look at the matter the other way round, and ask: Why in a community that possesses Mark should there arise the need for a Gospel like that of Matthew? the answer is less difficult to find. Indeed most scholars, including Butler, though not, of course, Farmer, hold that there is no doubt that Luke was produced in just such circumstances, i.e. that the Lucan community possessed Mark; and I myself would agree that there are no particularly compelling reasons for denying that the author of Luke knew Mark. In any case, whatever be the truth about the origins of Luke, it would clearly be quite reasonable for the author of Matthew (whom I shall henceforward, simply for convenience, refer to as Matthew)[18] to do what Streeterian orthodoxy says that he did, namely combine the brief text of Mark with whatever other material he had,[19] and thus produce a more complete account of Jesus from birth (or before) to Resurrection. So from the point of view of the needs of a particular community it looks as though the Markan priorist is on firmer ground - unless it can be shown that it is unlikely that Matthew did, in fact, have a text of Mark in front of him when he wrote or that he was necessarily influenced by such a text directly or indirectly.

In the end, there will be no substitute for commenting on the theoretical arguments for Markan priority and looking at the texts of Matthew and Mark again to see how far internal evidence points towards either one of them depending on the other; but before making a start on that potentially endless examination, I should at least comment on one or two further axioms and dogmas of Synoptic scholarship.

(1) First of all the matter of date. If we accept, as I do, that Luke and Acts are, as they show on their face, written by the same author, we presumably have to place Mark before the earliest reasonable date for Luke-Acts. Assuming that Luke precedes Acts, and noting that Acts ends with the imprisonment, but not the death of Paul in Rome, should we not

assume that Luke must have been written not much later than A.D. 64?

There seem to be only two specific objections to such a date: (i) that when Luke speaks of Jerusalem being 'surrounded by armies' (21:20), he knew that such a thing had occurred under Vespasian and Titus; (ii) that in Luke's version of the Beatitudes (6:22) we read 'they exclude you ($\dot{\alpha}\phi o\rho\acute{\iota}\sigma\omega\sigma\iota\nu$) and revile you and cast out ($\dot{\epsilon}\kappa\beta\acute{\alpha}\lambda\omega\sigma\iota\nu$) your name as evil', where Matthew has 'they revile you and persecute you and speak every evil against you' (5:11). The former language is sometimes said to indicate that Luke is referring to the Birkath-ha-Minim, the curse upon Christians in the synagogues that was formally instituted in the eighties, after Jamnia.[20] Such an interpretation, however, is the merest guess. Luke's language does not necessarily indicate the post-Jamnian situation; it could perfectly well describe what regularly happened to Paul and other missionaries. As for Vespasian and Titus we should notice that Luke does not state that Jerusalem has fallen, only that it is besieged. The passage might even be taken as evidence for Luke's writing *before* the fall of Jerusalem in 70 but after the beginning of the Jewish War in 66. But such an explanation is not essential. Luke, who tends to prefer the homely to the high-flown, might have simply preferred to rewrite the language of Danielic prophecy, the 'abomination of desolation', in terms more intelligible to Gentiles.

We may conclude that there is no good reason to date Luke much after the mid-sixties - unless we are certain that Luke also knew Matthew, and that Matthew has a substantially later date. But we cannot yet assume either that Luke knew Matthew, or, more importantly in our argument, that Matthew itself is later than A.D. 65.

Hence, at the present stage of our enquiry we have to maintain that Mark is probably to be dated in the early sixties,[21] unless we assume that Luke wrote a first draft (Proto-Luke), came across Mark's text later on, and then reworked his draft to include the Markan material.[22] There are, of course, enormous difficulties in that hypothesis, not the least of them being that Luke's rewriting must have involved recasting his whole original project in a Markan framework, for Luke seems in general to have fitted blocks of non-Markan material into a Markan frame.

Leaving aside, therefore, the hypothetical and unjustified rewriting of Luke by Luke, we have to find Mark to have been written some time before the mid-sixties, for he is available for use by Luke at about that time. Indeed a date somewhere between 60 and 65 for Mark is generally acceptable to modern scholarship, and more or less accords - for what that is worth - with the ancient testimony that Mark was written by Mark either after the deaths of Peter and Paul (Irenaeus),[23] or during Peter's lifetime (Clement of Alexandria).[24] Now if we turn to Matthew, we observe that

Markan priorists are bound to find a date later than that of Mark, but if we regard the question of the priority of these two Gospels as still open, very little remains in the way of argument for fixing Matthew to the period after A.D. 70. Indeed the only substantial argument that remains is another version of the claim about Jamnia: this time it is argued that *Matthew* reflects the split between Church and Synagogue that was then more or less formalized.[25] But again this claim is not as strong as it has sometimes appeared.[26] The Pauline letters give ample independent evidence of hostility to Christians in synagogues well before A.D. 70 - quite enough to account for the anti-Jewish sections of Matthew, even if we take no account of possible additions and variations to the original Matthaean text. And if we wish to discuss the basic relationships between Christianity and other forms of Judaism in Palestine before the fall of Jerusalem, we can hardly forget the evidence of the *events* of the Gospels[27] - not to mention the death of Stephen and the subsequent persecution described in Acts (8:1), the killing of James, brother of John, by Herod (Acts 12:2), and the actions of the Sadducaean high-priest Ananas in A.D. 62 in securing the death of James the 'brother of the Lord'.[28]

In fact what seems to be the convincing argument for a date for Matthew after A.D. 70 is merely the assertion that Matthew depends on Mark. Remove that assertion and the date for Matthew becomes uncertain. It is incredible, for example, that scholars should claim that it was impossible for Jesus to predict the destruction of the Temple (Mt 24:1 - 3, Mk 13:1 - 4, Lk 21:5 - 7), or that the reference to the 'abomination of desolation' (Mt 24:15, Mk 13:14; cf. Lk. 21:20) must be a *post eventum* prophecy, that is, a 'prophecy' attributed to Jesus after the event had occurred, but not actually uttered by him. Accusations about the destruction of the Temple were among the charges levelled against Jesus before the Sanhedrin (Mt 26:61, Mk 14:58). Perhaps these too can be dismissed as later invention, but the ice is getting thinner! And is it altogether absurd to suggest that an intelligent Jew, soaked in the traditions of the Old Testament, could have uttered such forecasts of doom? Others besides Jesus had done so.[29]

Neither references to persecution of Christians in synagogues, nor references to the predicted destruction of the Temple give us much to go on in determining a date for Matthew. Nor again does talk of Matthew's supposed ecclesiastical interests. Form critics are sometimes inclined to assume that references to a 'Church' (Mt 16:18 and 18:17), or indeed to any organization of the believers, must be anachronistic. Yet this is a very curious view to take. It assumes that Jesus could not have imagined (or presumably desired) that his followers should remain together after his death - a wholly question-begging proposition. And let us look briefly at Mt 18:15ff. in a little more detail. Jesus says that if a brother sins, you must try to reprove him patiently, but 'if he refuses to listen . . . tell it to the Church'. And if that is of no avail, 'let him be to you as the Gentile and the tax-collector'. Probably a very appropriate saying for Jesus at this stage of his ministry: the 'Church' is for Jews only - a matter to which we shall return in a later discussion of the Syrophoenician woman.

Of course, the question of later strands of material arises here. This section about the Church *could* be an interpolation into earlier material, given a bogus attribution to Jesus. Such arguments can always be used to rid ourselves of inconvenient material, but we cannot get very far along these lines. For even if the word 'Church' or its Aramaic equivalent is alien to Jesus, even if the *concept* of an organization of believers is similarly alien, we have absolutely no idea of when it first came into existence. In any case Matthew's Gospel was written several years after Jesus' death, presumably when even the term 'Church' could well have been current, but we have no means of reaching any kind of chronological precision.

In brief there is as yet no convincing evidence that Irenaeus was wrong when, perhaps paraphrasing or rewriting Papias, he declared that Matthew's Gospel was written while Peter and Paul were gospelling in Rome and laying the foundations of the Church.[30] Of course if Irenaeus were entirely accurate, he would have to be accepted in a further particular; that Matthew wrote earlier than Mark. But we should notice that Irenaeus does not say that Mark knew Matthew's work. We must leave these problems of chronology aside for the present.

(2) The second preliminary matter which demands discussion, however brief, is the alleged document Q. We recall that the classical theory in Synoptic criticism is that Matthew and Luke used Mark and supplemented it both with material unique to each of themselves and with a second common document. This document, originally thought to be a collection of the sayings of Jesus, was supposed to account for the material common to Matthew and Luke, but absent from Mark. A number of scholars, including Streeter,[31] believed that it was represented in a more pure form by Luke than by Matthew, since it can be observed that whereas Matthew seems to be in the habit of blending Markan with non-Markan material,[32] Luke prefers to operate with blocks. Hence the Q-blocks in Luke are more or less pure Q. Other Two-Documentarians, however, doubt this result: Burney, for example, comments that 'If we admit that parallelism is a sign of originality, we must assign to Matthew the palm for having (at least in such cases as can be tested by this criterion) preserved the sayings of "Q" in a more original form than Luke'.[33]

But arguments about whether Matthew or Luke preserves a better text
of Q are secondary to the question of whether Q ever existed, and if it did
exist, what it contained. Those who disliked the Q-theory used to be able
to claim that there is no evidence that written collections of sayings ever
actually existed, and that their supporters often fell back on misinter-
preting Papias' talk about *logia*.[34] Furthermore, they objected, if there
were such collections, why did they disappear so rapidly and without trace?
The question of the disappearance may still raise problems, but we do now
know that at some stage, and probably at least as early as the first half of
the second century, there were people who produced such sayings-collec-
tions: the Gospel of Thomas, which probably dates from not long after
A.D. 140, is an example.[35] But the discovery of this document at Nag-
Hammadi is not of immediate help in our present problems. In general it
seems likely that Thomas depends on the canonical Gospels,[36] particularly
Matthew and Luke, rather than that it is their source. However, there are
certain *logia* which may derive from an original and independent tradition
(e.g. 31, 32, 33). Perhaps more important, however, is the matter of
Thomas' use of parables. All the parables that are collected by Matthew
in his thirteenth chapter occur in the Gospel of Thomas, but they are scat-
tered throughout the Gospel and the interpretations provided by Matthew
are not given. Now we know that Matthew collects material on similar
themes and groups it together. A comparison of Thomas' parables with
those in the thirteenth chapter of Matthew, therefore, might suggest that
Thomas was using a source also available to Matthew. If this were so, there
would be evidence, perhaps from the first century A.D., of the existence of
a sayings-collection which might be a candidate for the label Q. But we
must repeat that it is not certain that Thomas did use Matthew's source
rather than Matthew. Other reasons for the scattering of parables throughout a Gospel might be adduced.

So we are still not in a position to determine whether there were or were
not written collections of sayings circulating when Matthew and Luke were
being written. More basic, however, is the problem that there are many
good reasons for thinking that Q, whatever it was, must have been something more than a sayings-source. Recently Butler,[37] Farrer[38] and others
have in fact suggested that Q seems to expand so much as to become indis-
tinguishable from Matthew. Thus the sources of Luke would include not
Mark and Q, but Mark and Matthew. This is a solution to which we can
return later; let it suffice for the moment to say that there are considerable difficulties involved in supposing that Luke has knowledge of Matthew.[39]
What I rather want to emphasize is that if Q seems able to expand from a
sayings-source to - in the opinion of some - the virtual equivalent of Matthew,

there should also be grave doubts as to the likelihood of Q being a single document. In 1911 Streeter believed that not only Matthew and Luke, but also Mark, were dependent on Q,[40] and he cited a number of texts, of which the Beelzeboul controversy (Mk 3:23-30 and parallels) is among the most persuasive, as proof of it. In 1924, however, he argued that Matthew had assimilated Mark to Q in these passages, and that Mark and Q are each independent of the other.[41] Streeter's manoeuvres seem designed merely as different ways of avoiding an unpleasant alternative, for there is non-Markan material common to Matthew and Luke (and agreements of Matthew and Luke against Mark) which he thought could be explained by some sort of derivation from a common source or by Luke following Matthew; but for Streeter the second alternative was impossible. If we opt for the common source, however, we are in considerable difficulties about what other material that source contained apart from what is in our Matthew and Luke. Q may, or may not, have contained large parts of Mark which also appear in the Triple Tradition (Matthew and Luke as well as Mark), or even other material of which no record has come down to us. And, as we implied above, Q may be more than one document. That is sometimes admitted. But if it is, how do we determine the nature of all or any of these documents? The answers are many and varied.[42]

Let us concentrate on one respect in which the question of Q (whatever he or she may be) is relevant to the problem of the relationship between Mark and Matthew. If there was no Q, how do we explain those passages where Matthew seems to preserve the more original tradition - and few would now deny that there are a number of such passages? If there was no Q, that is no document separate from Mark and Matthew, then it looks as though these passages point towards the dependence of Mark on Matthew as the more original text, with all the difficulties that entails. Unless, of course, we suppose that Matthew had access in Markan passages to non-documentary material - which, of course, he must have had. Styler commented,[43] 'If Matthew had access to a non-Marcan source, then there is no problem for advocates of Marcan priority. Q is therefore relevant, since it is just what is required - i.e. a non-Marcan source.' That is certainly true, but it gets us nowhere on the question of what Q was, and above all it assumes, which Styler and many others regularly assume, that Q (the non-Markan source for Matthew where Matthew parallels Luke) is a written document (or documents?) with, so to speak, a beginning, middle and end, or at least a specific purpose. But if in fact Q were unwritten material, then the 'primitivity' of particular *Markan* passages in Matthew's version proves nothing about the relationship between the two Gospels, or the dependence

of one on the other, for once we admit that Matthew is regularly using unwritten, i.e. traditionally handed down material, there is nothing to stop
us supposing that both Matthew and Mark preserve sections and versions
of that same deposit. For if material shared by Matthew and Luke, but not
found in Mark, derives from oral tradition, it is hard to argue that Matthew
would hold that material in such low esteem that he would *always* reject it
in favour of Mark in Markan passages. Of course most students of the
Synoptic Problem would cry halt at this point. It is, they say, an axiom of
Synoptic criticism that although oral tradition might explain the divergences in the Synoptics, only literary derivation can explain the similarities. We must refrain from comment on this at this stage.

Of course, to say that Matthew and Mark preserve the same deposit is
not to say that they derive from an original Ur-Markus, which Mark preserves more faithfully than Matthew. Nor is it necessarily to admit a Proto-
Matthew available as a written source both for canonical Matthew and for
Mark. It is merely to say that of the available traditions about Jesus,
Matthew has selected some identical with those selected by Mark, some
more distantly related and others additional. Reasons will be required to
account for the similarities, particularly the similarities of order, but also
those of material, among the traditions selected. But as to the total amount
of source material available, it may be as well to quote the last words of
John (21:25): 'But there are also many other things which Jesus did; were
every one of them to be written, I suppose that the world itself could not
contain the books that could be written.'

At this point it is necessary to revert briefly to the question of whether
Luke knew Matthew. It is sometimes said that the alternatives are either
that Luke knew Matthew or that he knew Q, for where else would he get
the material which is neither peculiar to himself nor clearly borrowed from
Mark, but which is shared with Matthew? Now, as we have already hinted,
it need not follow that if Luke did not know Matthew, he must know a
single written document in 'Q-passages'. Luke himself tells us (1:1) that
there existed many written sources for the events connected with Jesus,
and he adds that the originators of these various accounts were those who
from the beginning were eyewitnesses and 'ministers of the word'.[44] In
other words accounts were handed down to Luke's generation, including
Luke himself, and some of those who heard them wrote them down. The
only reasonable exegesis of this is that there were both written and unwritten accounts of Jesus' activities available to Luke. In view of this explicit statement, there seems to be little basis for deciding *a priori* whether,
in the passages which Luke shares with Matthew only, (i) Luke follows
Matthew, or (ii) Luke draws on an oral source (or sources) also available to

Matthew (and perhaps to Mark?), or (iii) Luke shares a common written
source (or sources) with Matthew. And other permutations may also be
possible.

Despite frequent assertion to the contrary, it is no argument against
Luke borrowing from Matthew to point out that Luke has changed Matthew's
order, for it is clear that in general it is Mark's order, not Matthew's or anyone else's that Luke follows. Nor need the problem of the possible originality of certain Lucan passages detain us long, for it is certain that Matthew
and Mark are not Luke's only possible sources; and even in passages like
'Blessed are you poor' (Lk 6:20) and 'Blessed are the poor in spirit' (Mt 5:3),
were Luke's version demonstrably more original, authentic, or whatever,[45]
that still would not show that in such comparatively rare cases Luke may
not have modified Matthew in the light of what he regarded as a better tradition which he had available. A *common* source is not necessary to explain
the phenomena in question. Nevertheless it should be clearly stated that
there is at least one particularly serious problem to be solved if we want to
regard Matthew as a direct source for Luke. Why is it that where Luke has
chosen to follow Mark, he consistently prefers him to Matthew (if it is
Matthew)? And the problem of order comes in here too. It is not Matthew's
order but Mark's which Luke consistently follows. Clearly he has taken a
decision, as a matter of policy, that where Mark is available, he is consistently to be preferred to the 'Matthaean' source (though not always to
others). Now there may be good reasons for this, such as that he thought
that Mark represented the teaching of Peter, but even that is scarcely adequate to account for his near-absolute preference for Mark and for Mark's
order, *if he had Matthew available*.[46] For all that we know of Christian
antiquity leads us to suppose that whatever weaknesses we may see in
Matthew's descriptions of events in Jesus' life, the ancients were unaware
of them: they liked Matthew's Gospel. Why then did Luke so frequently
avoid it when he could use Mark, but accord it such importance elsewhere?[47]

In fairness to the proponents of Luke's use of Matthew, it must be admitted that there are indeed a number of passages where it would seem
that to bring in a written Q or Qs is unnecessary.[48] I do not intend, however, to pursue the problem further at this point, but merely to observe
again that both Streeter and his followers, and Butler and his (along with
countless others who have offered hypotheses about the Synoptics), make
the fundamental assumption that in trying to isolate whether there is or is
not a Q which is the source of Luke (as previously of Matthew), we are
dealing only with the possible existence of written documents. Both sides
in the debate reduce the possible influence of an oral tradition to virtually
zero, and even neglect the possibility seemingly suggested by Luke himself
in his preface of an interplay between oral and written sources.

Let us leave Luke aside and return to more basic matters. It is now generally agreed that the only legitimate approach to the question of the relation of Matthew to Mark is the detailed comparison of their material. I have already suggested that there is one serious ground for concern for the advocates of the dependence of Mark on Matthew: that is, if Matthew existed, why write Mark? Nevertheless, it has been suggested that, although Matthaean priority seems incredible, it must be accepted as the proper deduction from internal evidence. Above all, the argument has tended to turn on whether Mark or Matthew preserves the more primitive account, and whether it can be shown that one or the other of them has doctored this primitive account (or accepted a doctored account from others) in the interests of church politics, inconvenient theology, liturgical development or whatever. Needless to say investigators run the risk of knowing too much *a priori* about these matters, and of deriving such 'knowledge' from Mark or Matthew themselves by various forms of circular argument. And what, in fact, is primitivity?

Once upon a time people thought that there were a number of tests that could easily be applied to determine the pearls of original Christian teaching and to separate them from the accretion of garbage, sometimes disguising itself as picturesque fable, but of an unpleasantly Judaistic or Hellenistic origin, which often accompanies them in our Gospel traditions. Some of the tests were roughly along the following lines:

(i) More miracles or miraculous additions means later.
(ii) 'Crude' healing miracles involving the use of saliva, recorded by Mark (7:32-6, 8:22-6),[49] but omitted by Matthew and Luke, indicate a process of bowdlerization.
(iii) Interesting and picturesque details, such as Jesus sleeping on a cushion (Mk 4:38, omitted in Matthew), are reflections of the work of an early eyewitness.
(iv) An increase in the number of 'respectful' references to Jesus, and a purging of passages suggesting his weakness or inadequacy, are signs of lateness.

There are other approaches to the problem; unfortunately none of them is reliable. We have now been taught to recognize that tendencies in these matters are not strong enough to warrant the name of laws.[50] No *a priori* assertions are possible; all texts have to be judged on their individual merits. There is no scientific basis for assertions that either Mark or Matthew is regularly the more primitive. And even the 'more primitive' is not necessarily the earlier.

The tricky matter of primitivity is not the only guide we have for an

internal examination of Mark and Matthew.[51] Discussion of primitivity
must go hand in hand with a necessary exercise of the imagination. I propose to examine a great variety of parallel texts in Matthew and Mark, and
to attempt to understand Matthew's text on the hypothesis that he had
Mark available, and Mark's text on the hypothesis that he had Matthew. Of
course, there is also the possibility of the indirect influence of the one on
the other, but once we allow for that, we must remember that it has been
assumed that very special conditions are required to account for the
similarities in the Synoptic tradition, conditions, apparently, that rule out
the predominant influence of oral tradition. When we get into indirect literary influence, these special conditions may not exist; perhaps it is an
awareness of that which has induced most scholars to think only of direct
influences.

What is needed is an investigation into whether what we find in particular sections of the canonical Gospels of Matthew and Mark is intelligible in
the light of direct influence either way. This stage of the discussion will be
mainly, but not entirely, limited to the so-called Markan passages of
Matthew and the comparable material in Mark. I shall pay particular atten
tion to details of wording and to the matter of the ordering of the pericopae.
In regard to the latter I shall place considerable emphasis on two points:
(1) that general agreements of order do not necessarily presuppose detailed
agreements about order within the pericopae; and (2) that, as Antonio
Gaboury has explained and argued at great length, [52] it must be clearly recognized that, roughly speaking, whereas in the narrative from the appearance of John the Baptist to the Temptation (Mt 3:1 - 4:11 and parallels),
and from the passage where Herod thinks that Jesus is John the Baptist
risen from the dead to the description of the Empty Tomb (Mt 14:1 -
28:10), Matthew and Mark seem to agree very substantially in order,
Mt 4:12 - 13:58 contains considerable divergencies of order even among
the pericopae themselves. As Gaboury recognizes, the only possible deductions from this latter fact are either that Matthew (or Mark) was particularly concerned to follow Mark (or Matthew) in one section but less concerned in the other, or, more radically, that at some stage *before* the appearance of our canonical texts the narrative in some parts of the tradition about
Jesus was already very much more firmly secured in its basic order and
structure. And a general corollary of this is that 'global' statistics about
the whole of Mark or Matthew are likely to be misleading.

Before proceeding further, however, I should like to discuss two preliminary but important matters related to the subject of the order of the
Synoptic pericopae. It is usually assumed that the phenomenon to be
explained is that Matthew and Luke very rarely agree on matters of order

against Mark. It is then argued that the dependence of Matthew and Luke on Mark is the only way to explain this situation. But in fact the dependence on Mark of Luke alone would satisfy within these terms of reference, if Matthew and Mark both depended on a common source or a common fixed tradition. For in these circumstances Luke would normally agree with both Matthew and Mark in the 'Triple Tradition', and where he diverged from Matthew he would normally agree with Mark since it seems to be Mark's order (or the order represented by Mark) which he regards as authoritative.

But beyond this situation there is a more basic set of facts which seems to me to have received too little attention from students of the Synoptics. Anyone producing a Synoptic Gospel had a considerable part of his sequence pre-arranged. Thus the preaching of John the Baptist must precede the teaching of Jesus, the Galilean mission must precede the last journey to Jerusalem, the trial of Jesus must precede his execution. Thus arguments from order to literary dependence ought to be based on parallels of order outside this basic framework as well as on the framework itself. And among those passages where parallels in ordering may be found, we should expect to find a particularly high degree of verbal similarity as well. Now an inspection of any Synopticon - Farmer's multicoloured one is particularly useful for this purpose[53] - will indicate that the number of sections (or parts of sections) where all three Synoptics are *both* parallel in order *and* contain a high percentage of near-identical vocabulary is limited. The following list is certainly more or less complete.

John the Baptist (Mk 1:1 - 4, 7 and parallels)
The Healing of a Leper (Mk 1:40 - 4 and parallels)
The Healing of the Paralytic (Mk 2:5 - 11 and parallels)
The Call of Levi (Mk 2:14 - 17 and parallels)
The Question about Fasting (Mk 2:18 - 22 and parallels)
Plucking Ears of Grain on the Sabbath (Mk 2:23 - 8 and parallels)
The Parable of the Sower (Mk 4:3 - 9 and parallels)
The Reason for Speaking in Parables (Mk 4:10 - 12 and parallels)
The Interpretation of the Sower (Mk 4:13 - 20 and parallels) (?)
The Feeding of the Five Thousand (Mk 6:35 - 44 and parallels)
The Confession at Caesarea Philippi (Mk 8:27 - 31 and parallels)
Conditions of Discipleship (Mk 8:34 - 9:1 and parallels)
The Transfiguration (Mk 9:2 - 7 and parallels)
The Dispute about Greatness (Mk 9:36 - 7 and parallels)
Blessing the Children (Mk 10:13 - 15 and parallels)
The Rich Young Man (Mk 10:17 - 31 and parallels)
The Entry into Jerusalem (Mk 11:1 - 3 and parallels)

The Question about Authority (Mk 11:27 - 33 and parallels)
The Parable of the Wicked Tenants (Mk 12:1 - 12 and parallels)
The Question about Tribute to Caesar (Mk 12:13 - 17 and parallels)
The Question about the Resurrection (Mk 12:18 - 27 and parallels)
David's Son (Mk 12:35 - 7 and parallels)
The Prediction of the Destruction of the Temple and parts of the
    Synoptic Apocalypse (Mk 13:1 - 18, 25 - 6 and parallels)
The Parable of the Fig Tree (Mk 13:28 - 9 and parallels)
The Time of the Parousia (Mk 13:30 - 1 and parallels)
Preparation for the Passover (Mk 14:12 - 16 and parallels)
The Traitor (Mk 14:20 - 1 and parallels)
The Institution (Mk 14:22 - 5 and parallels)
In the Garden and the Arrest (Mk 14:36 - 8, 43, 46 - 8 and parallels)
The Crucifixion (Mk 15:22 - 33 and parallels)

What does this set of passages add up to? First of all we notice that there are far more passages from the latter part of Mark than from the earlier, more, that is, from that section which Gaboury recognized as exhibiting a more fixed order and which he labelled C ('commun'). Secondly let us analyse the collection of texts which we have. The whole set can be summarized as follows:

The Announcement of Jesus	(Introduction)
Two Healings ⎤	Section D
The Call of Levi ⎟	(Gaboury's 'différent')
Two Problems of the Law ⎦	
The Declaration of Jesus as the Messiah ⎤	
and the Prediction of the Passion ⎟	
Three approaches to the Question of ⎟	
Who is in Favour with God ⎟	
The Entry into Jerusalem ⎟	Section C
The End of the Old Order and the ⎟	
New Dispensation ⎟	
The Passover ⎟	
The Conspiracy against Jesus and its ⎟	
Effects ⎦	

Section C, beginning with a prefiguring of the Eucharist (The Feeding of the 5000) is almost wholly governed by a sequence of events which is logical and would have some claim to being historical. Section D gives the briefest possible survey of Jesus' work (healing, calling, using parables), and finally establishes his relationship to the Old Covenant. In brief we may suggest that if there were any kind of basic tradition about Jesus, chronological in nature but firmly centred on his Passion, this set of material would be it. Is it too much to suppose that such a sequence and much of the common matter it contains could be held in the memory?

2

THE LITERARY HYPOTHESIS:
SOME PRELIMINARY TESTS
(Mt 3:1 - 9:17)

Antonio Gaboury listed Mt 3:1 - 4:11 as part of his section C, that is as
material that was more worked over before it reached the Synoptic writers
themselves. He thought that Luke knew this material at a more primitive
stage of its development than did Mark and Matthew.[54] Mt 4:12 - 9:17
he included in his section D, and he thought that Matthew knew this material at a more primitive stage than Mark and Luke. We may bear these
theories in mind as we look at Mt 3:1 - 9:17, but we need not regard the
claims to primitivity as guidelines in our own enquiry. We shall, however,
take note of the fact, to which we alluded in the previous chapter, that
some parts of this section of Matthew fall into that comparatively limited
amount of Synoptic material where similarity of order among the pericopae
coincides with a close verbal similarity in the texts of the different Gospels.
Our intention in this chapter will simply be to begin that exercise of imagination to which we pointed earlier, and to attempt to ascertain whether
the variations in the tradition as it is rendered by Matthew and by Mark
seem particularly intelligible in the light of direct literary derivation. We
shall be wondering, in fact, whether theories of literary derivation seem to
account for the phenomena with such a high degree of probability that one
or other of them must be correct. In the course of our discussion of both
this and subsequent sections of the text of the Synoptics, we shall inevitably
be considering Luke as well as Matthew and Mark. Information of various
kinds will thus be forthcoming about Luke, but it will be limited in scope,
and our comments on Luke will primarily be concerned with the way in
which Luke may help us understand the relationship between Matthew
and Mark.

1. John the Baptist
One of the more striking features of Matthew is that at certain points in
the narrative there are rather abrupt stops and starts. Matthew makes
little attempt in a number of places to make his text smooth. A significant
example of this phenomenon occurs at the end of chapter 2. Matthew has
just completed his account of Mary and Joseph settling in Nazareth and

refers to the 'prophecy', 'He shall be called a Nazarene'. After this there
begins a Markan section of narrative, introduced only by the vague, if not
in this case actually misleading words, 'in those days'. This certainly looks
as though at the beginning of the Markan material Matthew has shifted
over to a new source. Presumably his old source or sources had nothing
to fill the interval between the return of Jesus with Mary and Joseph to
Nazareth and the preaching of John the Baptist. Mark, of course, begins
with John the Baptist, and Luke has a new beginning at this point: 'In
the fifteenth year of the reign of Tiberius Caesar'. Literary dependence is
an obvious explanation of the gap, and Markan priorists could assert that
Luke has made a better join of his non-Markan to his Markan material
than Matthew. But the first question is: Is the second source necessarily
Mark? Certainly Mark begins at this point, so one can probably assume
that much of the early preaching of the gospel began with John the
Baptist.[55] But the question clearly is: Do Matthew (and Luke) use Mark,
or do they depend on the tradition (written or unwritten) on which Mark
is also based? In approaching this problem we shall look at Matthew's
account in some detail and compare it with Mark's, but first we should
make a methodological point.

If we accept that the preaching about Jesus began with an account of
John the Baptist, we have good reason to recognize what is in any case
likely, that the sources for the Nativity narratives of Matthew and of Luke are
recherché. The early preachers were probably not particularly concerned
with this material. If Luke had Matthew before him, he did not think it
necessary to include even some of the highly interesting texts (such as the
account of the Magi) which he found there. And if Q were to be defined
as the non-Markan material common to Matthew and Luke, we should observe that this supposed document did not contain the Nativity material
either. In antiquity generally it must be admitted that there is little concern with a hero's childhood, and however difficult it may be for us to
accept, we must recognize that the same attitude may have characterized
the early Christians. It has been plausibly speculated that it became necessary to add in what could be gleaned about Jesus' birth only when stories of
his illegitimacy began to be put about among the Jews. And of his childhood all we have canonically is the story of his visit to the Temple at the
age of twelve given by Luke.

Bearing in mind then that we should not necessarily assume that
Matthew picked up his copy of Mark and found that it began with John
the Baptist, but that the preaching of Jesus, *and therefore a whole series
of traditions about Jesus,* began with an account of John, let us look in
more detail at the Synoptic versions. As we have already observed,

Mt 3:1 - 6, Mk 1:1 - 6 and Lk 3:1 - 6 are in many respects, including verbally, very close to one another: the prophet Isaiah is named and quoted, though in different amounts; there are a number of exact verbal parallels. Yet at the same time the *order* within the section is not fixed, even when the words are identical. Matthew, for instance, describes John the Baptist's clothing immediately after the quotation from Isaiah, while Mark does not and Luke omits the point altogether. It is not easy to see why either Mark or Matthew would decide to change their received order at this point. Perhaps, though only perhaps, more significant, is that whereas Mark and Luke indicate that John preached repentance for the forgiveness of sins (εἰς ἄφεσιν ἁμαρτιῶν), Matthew simply indicates that when John's disciples were baptized they confessed their sins (3:6) as a response to John's call to 'Repent, for the kingdom of heaven is at hand' (3:1).[56] Repentance seems to be especially emphasized in Matthew's account:[57] in verse 11 he includes it with 'I baptize you with water', etc., where Mark and Luke omit it.

We are beginning to observe some ways in which Matthew's account diverges, not always explicably in terms of written variants, from Mark. Let us now briefly go back to Mark himself and consider the matter of literary polish. Mark suddenly introduces us to John baptizing as to a man of whom we have previously heard nothing. Matthew's version is a little less abrupt; at least John is introduced at the beginning of the section - formally presented as it were. But again we are told nothing of his origins. Luke, on the other hand, has had a good deal about John in his Nativity narrative, so we know who he is even without Luke's more recent re-identification of him as son of Zechariah. Both Mark and Matthew look less literary here, and we recognize in general that Luke's Gospel is a more 'literary' composition. The form of Mark and Matthew seems less worked over. Perhaps Matthew's presentation is less bald than Mark's, but the difference may not be particularly significant. Perhaps indeed the difference may be so slight that it is hard to attribute it to a literary manipulation of a previous literary text. With this doubt in our minds we should be particularly attentive to any agreements in this passage between Matthew and Luke against Mark.

Thus far we have noted that Matthew and Mark appear to be less literary in their presentation of John the Baptist, and that there are a few agreements between Mark and Luke against Matthew. Let us see how this seemingly orthodox situation is affected by the later parts of the treatment of John, and in particular by the accounts of the baptism of Jesus. Now we know from the existence of Mt 3:7 - 10 and Lk 3:7 - 14 that both Matthew and Luke have non-Markan material, possibly from more than one source, available. Mt 3:11 - 12 and Lk 3:16 - 17 contain both agreements of these two Gospels against Mark and evidence suggesting that such agreements do not necessarily entail the use of Matthew by Luke; in other words that in addition to the possible influence of Mark there are at least two further sources needed to account for our texts of Matthew and Luke.

The peculiar nature of this section was clear to Streeter, who concluded that Mark and Q both gave independent witness to the narrative at this point. Mt 3:7 - 12 is a whole, he thought, of which Mk 1:7ff. is a mutilated fragment.[58] Streeter, as we have already mentioned, was in no doubt that the documentary source Q contained an account of John the Baptist; the problem he was concerned about was whether Mark knew Q or not. The obviously incomplete nature of Mark's account at this point doubtless impelled him towards his eventual conclusion that Mark and Q must be independent of one another. But the problem is more complicated, and we must attempt to ascertain whether a single source Q (or for that matter the use of Matthew by Luke as a supplement to Mark, or instead of Mark) is adequate to explain the phenomena. Mt 3:11 and Lk 3:16 agree against Mark in saying that the baptism of Jesus will be with the Holy Spirit *and with fire*. So presumably Q, if it existed, referred to fire. It has also long been recognized that Mt 3:12 and Lk 3:17 both begin with a relative pronoun referring to the previous verse - so that their source here could be identical. So far, then, it seems that we must say either that Luke knew Matthew or that they both used Q. But at this point we must turn our attention to the differences between Luke and Matthew in the Q passages. If we start at Mt 3:7 (Lk 3:7), we notice the following points, of varying importance:

(i) Luke omits the Pharisees and Sadducees of Mt 3:7. This may be dismissed as typical.

(ii) Luke derives his 3:10 - 14 neither from Mark nor Matthew, for they both omit it. It is clear then that Luke has at least three sources at his disposal dealing with John the Baptist, if he uses Matthew (i.e. Mark, Matthew and L) - unless we deny that he used Mark and attribute all his agreements with Mark against Matthew to L!

(iii) Matthew (3:11) speaks of John not being worthy to *carry* the sandals of the one who will come after, while Luke, agreeing with Mark, speaks of 'untying'. Yet Luke omits Mark's 'stoop down'. We might, of course, invoke textual corruption to get round these points, or mistranslations of an Aramaic original.

(iv) Matthew 3:14 - 15 may not be a Q passage, but it may be significant that Luke agrees with Mark against Matthew in

omitting John's initial reluctance to baptize Jesus at all.[59]
Perhaps the section is a later accretion, though this is unlikely.[60]
If it is not, then Luke, if he knows Matthew, has chosen to
suppress it. More likely, however, is that Luke is following
another source here, a source probably unknown to Matthew,
for Luke's verse immediately preceding his account of the
baptism of Jesus deals with a quite different event, namely
the arrest of John by Herod. Both Mark and Matthew refer
to this event, mentioned here by Luke quite out of its proper
chronological sequence, much later in their narratives
(Mk 6:17 - 18; Mt 14:3 - 4). In our present context it is
striking for Luke to diverge from the narrative sequence presented by Matthew and Mark, particularly if he had both of
them available. The most likely explanation is that Luke's
account of John the Baptist derives primarily, if not exclus-
ively, from a single source other than Mark and Matthew, but
overlapping both of them in many places. If this is correct, it
would reflect Luke's apparently usual pattern of using blocks
of material from a single source.

We began this discussion by pointing to some divergences between Mark
and Matthew. We now see by examining the relationship between Matthew
and Luke that the notion of a single source Q is beginning to dissolve. If
this is right, then that single source cannot be used to explain the variations
between Matthew and Mark. Clearly in these matters proof is impossible to
obtain, but we may be encouraged by our analysis to pursue the possibility
that in the accounts of John the Baptist neither the view that Mark summarized Matthew nor the alternative that Matthew assimilated Mark with Q
is adequate.

Some confirmation of these results may be found by looking at the pas-
sage dealing with the divine voice that 'confirmed' Jesus' baptism. In
Matthew the reading '*This* is my Son' is overwhelmingly supported. In
Mark there is similarly strong support for '*You* are my Son, in *you* . . .'.
Luke's text is less unanimously attested; indeed there is a 'Western' reading,
'You are my son and I have begotten you today', apparently deriving from
Psalm 2:7, and frequently quoted by patristic authors of the first three cen-
turies,[61] while a few witnesses serve up Matthew's 'This is my beloved Son'
by assimilation. Nevertheless the bulk of the evidence attributes the
Markan version to Luke. So some of our early impressions are vindicated
here: there is clear difference of opinion between the oldest texts of Mark
and Matthew that we can identify, with no trace of early assimilation. And

Luke, for whatever reason, has followed the Markan version. The passage seems to confirm the earlier impression that although Mark and Matthew present very similar accounts, including much verbal similarity, in the present narrative, there are significant differences which are hard to explain on the thesis that one Evangelist used the other.

We should notice that in the case of Mt 3:16 - 17, the Q theory breaks down altogether. It is clearly not the case that Matthew has assimilated Mark to a source Q which is better represented by Luke. There is no reason to think that Luke is following either Matthew's source or Matthew himself. The most likely explanation is that he is following a special source of his own - or assimilating that special source to Mark. The final possibility is that he is simply adapting Mark's text, having abandoned his special source after 3:21.

Sanders has pointed out that whereas it is usually the case that Matthew's version of a particular story is more abbreviated than Mark's, and that Mark usually seems to be the 'middle term', in Butler's phrase, between Matthew and Luke, in the account of John the Baptist the situation is different.[62] Mark is more abbreviated than Matthew, and Matthew seems to be the middle term between Mark and Luke. Our own examination of the passage differs somewhat from that of Sanders, but it has many points of similarity, especially the rejection of Q. The conclusions which we would wish to draw from the evidence are different too. Sanders, still working within the tradition that there are 'direct literary relationships among the Synoptic Gospels', thinks that the account of John the Baptist (and many other passages) points to the fact that relationships between the Gospels are very complex, wishing to argue for frequent 'overlapping' and cross-fertilization, as well as a knowledge by the Evangelists of overlapping traditions.[63] The thesis is obviously possible, and can only help in breaking down the stereotypes which are usually paraded. But consideration will also have to be given to a more radical alternative; that it is the literary-derivation theory which causes a good deal of the trouble, particularly the trouble in explaining the relationship of Matthew and Mark.

2. The Temptation (Mt 4:1 - 11, Mk 1:12 - 13, Lk 4:1 - 13)
We are still in Gaboury's section C, where he found that the Gospel narrative was comparatively more fixed in its order, and where he claimed that Luke knew the tradition at a more primitive stage. We are also in another section where Streeter, in his early days, found it necessary to claim that Mark knew Q, the source of the fuller accounts in Matthew and Luke. This section is also similar to the account of John the Baptist in that Mark's version is abbreviated compared with Matthew's, and in that if he has summarized Matthew, he has done so cavalierly, giving no

specifics of the Temptations at all. Proceeding differently from the pattern
in the Nativity narratives, Matthew and Luke give substantially the same
story (thus indicating a Q passage), though they vary the order of the temptations. Thus the passage has some claim to be in 'Markan context' and
other to be Q; and to get the best of both worlds it could be said that Mark
had access to, but made very little use of, a written Q.[64] The beginning
and end of Matthew's and Mark's accounts have some similarities, but there
are significant differences too; and Luke seems to agree with Matthew, thus
following either Matthew or a source similar to (or identical with) Matthew's.
In the opening and closing sections, for example, we notice the following:

Mt	Mk	Lk
ἀνήχθη	ἐκβάλλει	ἤγετο
πειρασθῆναι	πειραζόμενος	πειραζόμενος
ὑπὸ τοῦ	ὑπὸ τοῦ	ὑπὸ τοῦ
διαβόλου	Σατανᾶ	διαβόλου
καὶ ἰδοὺ ἄγγελοι	καὶ οἱ ἄγγελοι	
προσῆλθον καὶ	διηκόνουν αὐτῷ	
διηκόνουν αὐτῷ		

The difficulty in understanding the relationship between Mark and
Matthew in this passage is highlighted by the fact that Mark's account, in
addition to being almost intolerably brief, is unclear as to whether Jesus
fasted or not.[65] The 'ministering' of the angels seems to be an allusion to
the feeding of Elijah by ravens, and to imply a fast, but whereas Matthew
and Luke say that Jesus fasted, Mark does not. Mark's version is clearly
compressed, but compressed what? Butler thinks compressed Matthew,
but, if so, compressed very incompetently. Streeter too thinks Matthew
more primitive (appealing, of course, to Q),[66] on the inadequate grounds
that the richer story is likely to be the earlier. Butler certainly seems on
firm ground in saying that Matthew is not based on Mark here, though his
framework is vaguely 'Markan'; but there is little justification for his ar-
guing the converse, i.e. that Mark used Matthew. As we have already observed, if Mark was referring to a written source when he wrote, he has
made a remarkably (and uncharacteristically) poor job of reproducing it:
at least the fasting rated a mention. It is far more likely that Mark's source
here (as for the Baptism section?) is purely oral. Matthew's source could
be oral too, or a mixture of written and oral material, but if he has a written source it is certainly not Mark.

If this is correct, we have to assume that the fact that both Matthew and Mark refer to ministering angels at the end of their descriptions of the Temptation is accidental, but there is nothing unreasonable about such a supposition. Presumably many versions of the story could have referred to them. It is noteworthy, however, that Luke does not mention them at this point, or indeed anywhere else in his narrative. Sanders thinks that in the Temptation narrative, as in the account of the Baptist, Matthew is the middle term between Mark and Luke, and certainly Luke's omission of the ministering angels combined with his clear reference to fasting argues strongly against his following Mark. But it is not clear that he follows Matthew either. His version is broadly similar to Matthew's, though with significant variations both of order (the temptations are in a different sequence) and of wording.[67] It also, however, bears obvious marks of editorializing ('full of the holy spirit', 4:1; 'until an appropriate time', 4:12), which make Gaboury's notion that it is more primitive less likely. It must be admitted that Luke may be following Matthew on this occasion, but if he is, he is probably deliberately preferring him to Mark - a possible but not necessary procedure. The other alternative is that Matthew and Luke have the same source, but if so that source is not Mark. Since our primary concern is the relationship between Mark and Matthew we need not speculate further.

3. The First Preaching in Galilee

We now move to Gaboury's section D, in which it is claimed that at the time the Gospels of Matthew and Mark appeared, the 'canonical tradition' was much less firmly fixed, since the Synoptic Gospels exhibit more marked differences in the order of the pericopae. The explanations of this phenomenon are no doubt many and varied, not the least of them being, as we have noted, that unlike the early sections of Mark and the narrative from the First Confession at Caesarea Philippi to Jesus' Passion and Death, the Galilean ministry is not easily identifiable in terms of chronological sequence.

Matthew and Mark agree that after the Temptation, news came that John the Baptist had been arrested, and that Jesus moved to Galilee (Mt 4:12, Mk 1:14).[68] It might be argued that Matthew's account betrays a better understanding of what happened: Matthew understands, where Mark does not, that Jesus 'withdrew' (ἀνεχώρησεν); things may have looked dangerous after John's arrest. As in the story of John the Baptist and in the Temptation narrative, Matthew, or his source(s), is fuller and more coherent in this pericope. He goes on to tell us that Jesus left Nazareth and settled in Capernaum and in the land of Zebulun and Naphtali, thus gaining the opportunity to work in another quotation from

Isaiah (9:1 - 2). Luke, it should be noted, follows a different version (and a different order) here, moving after a vague sentence about teaching in synagogues to the rejection at Nazareth, which both Mark and Matthew place at the end, not the beginning, of the 'disorderly' Galilean section. Luke's order might well be a revised version of the historical sequence, for it might seem 'logical' for Jesus to start preaching in his home town. But let us follow Matthew and Mark.

Again Matthew's report *looks* (and again it must be emphasized how subjective this is) more primitive. Jesus' original proclamation in Matthew is 'Repent, for the kingdom of heaven is at hand' - exactly the teaching which Matthew attributes to John the Baptist. In other words in Matthew's account Jesus begins precisely where John left off; and this is highly intelligible if he hoped to win over people who previously had noticed the Baptist's preaching. Mark's version is more elaborate: Jesus, he says, preached the Gospel of God. His message is what Matthew says it was, but, says Mark, he added 'Believe in the Gospel of God',[69] and, 'The time is fulfilled'. Some might suppose that Matthew has abbreviated, others that Mark has expanded or editorialized. But even if our text of Mark is expanded, we have no guidance as to when the expansion occurred; it cannot be *assumed* that it was with the author of Mark. In general who is the more primitive here cannot be determined with certainty.

But if Matthew has abbreviated what he found in Mark, it should be noted that he has abbreviated the first words of preaching Jesus uttered. But Matthew is following Mark's order, it is asserted. True enough, but the question remains: is it because he found that order in Mark? Certainly the addition of the topographical data and the quotation from Isaiah indicate that Matthew had other material than Mark available for this passage. So did he have Mark?

4. Calling the First Disciples (Mt 4:18 - 22, Mk 1:16 - 20)
The accounts of Matthew and Mark are very close in this section, and both writers put it immediately after Jesus' initial proclamation, thereby differing sharply from Luke whose version (5:1 - 11) is certainly independent.[70] Considerations of order and of verbal similarity both seem to point to the influence of one literary text on another. We might hope, therefore, to find good evidence as to whether Matthew copied Mark or vice versa, but in fact it is impossible to identify priority. Both texts give a number of words of Jesus in identical form, but if either or both had access to a sayings-collection, this would be readily accounted for. If either one copied the other, it is not a scissors-and-paste job, but the character of the variations may be judged if we point out that perhaps the most significant is that Mark mentions the hired servants while Matthew

does not, and that Matthew alone adds that Simon is called Peter, a fact
to which Mark does not allude before a Triple Tradition passage in chapter
3 (the list of the Twelve). But what can be deduced from these variants
is precisely nothing.

5. The Sermon on the Mount (Mt 5 - 7)

I do not propose to discuss this section at any length. It is generally recognized that the 'Sermon' is a collection of material, of which Mark preserves a little and Luke the majority elsewhere. Matthew has chosen to
group this material (preceded by an 'intermediary' section (Mt 4:23 - 5) to
which we shall allude later) soon after the beginning of Jesus' ministry,
presumably intending it to contain some of the major themes to which
Jesus constantly returned during his mission in Galilee. Matthew's decision
with respect to this body of material seems eminently reasonable, but the
existence of the 'Sermon' in the form that we have it shows that, if he
followed Mark, he had no hesitation in treating the Markan structure very
cavalierly indeed, and that Mark, if he followed Matthew, was happy to
omit large sections of important material, such as the Beatitudes and the
Lord's Prayer, for no very evident reason. In any case, the fact that
Matthew returns to the Markan order after his long 'digression' tells us
nothing about the relationship between the two - except that they followed the same tradition in broad outlines. The following section, the
healing of a leper, is the first passage since the account of John the Baptist
where both words and order are close together in all three Synoptics, an
indication, as I observed in Chapter One, that we are probably here dealing
with a passage which was always quoted in the very simplest versions of
the traditions about Jesus, perhaps as a paradigmatic story of healing.

6. Capernaum and Gadara/Gergesa

After the call of the first disciples Mark goes on to events in Capernaum,
which, unlike Matthew (cf. 4.13), he has not mentioned up to this point.
He then relates (as does Luke) the healing of a man with an 'unclean
spirit' - a story which has some parallels significantly close to the account
of the Gadarene (or Gergesene) demoniac to justify discussion of both
happenings together. Matthew's placing of the Gadarene demoniacs
(8:28 - 34) is substantially different from Mark's and Luke's (Mk 5:1 - 20
and Lk 8:26 - 39), for both Mark and Luke attach the story directly to
Jairus' Daughter and place it shortly before the spot where (according to
Gaboury) radical divergences of order diminish with the description of
Herod supposing that Jesus is John the Baptist risen from the dead
(Mt 14:1, Mk 6:14, Lk 9:7).

Mark's and Luke's accounts of Jesus in the synagogue at Capernaum
are very close verbally (Mk 1:21 - 28, Lk 4:31 - 7), particularly in their

record of the words of Jesus. We note especially identical wording as follows:

Lk	Mk
καὶ ἀνέκραξε φωνῇ μεγάλη,	καὶ ἀνέκραξε λέγων,
Ἐα, τί ἡμῖν καὶ σοί, Ἰησοῦ	Τί ἡμῖν καὶ σοί, Ἰησοῦ
Ναζαρηνέ; ἦλθες ἀπολέσαι ἡμᾶς;	Ναζαρηνέ; ἦλθες ἀπολέσαι ἡμᾶς;
οἶδά σε τίς εἶ, ὁ ἅγιος	οἶδά σε τίς εἶ, ὁ ἅγιος
τοῦ θεοῦ· καὶ ἐπετίμησεν αὐτῷ	τοῦ θεοῦ· καὶ ἐπετίμησεν αὐτῷ
ὁ Ἰησοῦς λέγων, Φιμώθητι, καὶ	ὁ Ἰησοῦς λέγων, Φιμώθητι, καὶ
ἔξελθε ἀπ'αὐτοῦ	ἔξελθε ἐξ αὐτοῦ

Turning to the account of the Gadarene (or Gergesene) demoniacs, we note the following features:

(i) Matthew has two demoniacs where Mark and Luke have one (Mt 8:28 - 34);
(ii) the positioning of the story in Matthew differs from that of Mark and Luke;
(iii) Matthew's account, though in places very close verbally to Mark and Luke, is considerably abbreviated. In particular Matthew omits the sequel in which Mark and Luke mention the request (rejected by Jesus) of the demoniac to become a disciple.

Various explanations have been offered about the relation of these events to the events in Capernaum.[71] Some say that Matthew's two demoniacs at Gadara are a conflation of the Markan Gerasene[72] demoniac with the demoniac from Capernaum. But if so, someone (Matthew) has deliberately (and for no very obvious theological reason) scrapped the Capernaum story and deliberately botched the Gerasene. And if Mark knew Matthew, the same difficulties arise. Mark has deliberately separated the two demoniacs and landed one of them in Capernaum. Of course the solution may be that either Mark knew (or supposed) that Matthew was mistaken, or vice versa. But it may be more plausible to suppose that Matthew does not follow Mark (or know Mark?) on these matters, nor Mark Matthew.

Let us now look at the words of the demoniacs and compare them with those quoted from the passage about the Capernaum synagogue. They are as follows:

Mt	Mk	Lk
καὶ ἰδοὺ ἔκραξαν λέγοντες,	καὶ κράξας φωνῇ	ἰδὼν δὲ τὸν Ἰησοῦν
Τί ἡμῖν καὶ σοί, υἱὲ τοῦ	μεγάλῃ λέγει, Τί	ἀνακράξας προσέπεσεν
θεοῦ; ἦλθες ὧδε πρὸ καιροῦ	ἐμοὶ καὶ σοί,	αὐτῷ καὶ φωνῇ μεγάλῃ
βασανίσαι ἡμᾶς;	Ἰησοῦ υἱὲ τοῦ θεοῦ	εἶπεν, Τί ἐμοὶ καὶ σοί,
	τοῦ ὑψίστου; ὁρκίζω	Ἰησοῦ υἱὲ τοῦ θεοῦ
	σε τὸν θεόν, μὴ	τοῦ ὑψίστου; δέομαί
	με βασανίσῃς	σου, μὴ
		με βασανίσῃς

There is no doubt that the Gadarene/Gergesene stories are basically similar in all three Synoptics. Unless we hold that Mark split up Matthew or that Matthew produced an amalgamated Mark, we must assume that the story came down in at least two versions. The common element in the story is the actual words of the demoniac(s), and these appear in all three Gospels. Mark and Luke are very close, though Luke is certainly not an exact copy of Mark throughout the whole narrative. The oddity is that the exact words of the demoniac occur again in Mark and Luke in the Capernaum synagogue. There is no particular reason why two demoniac stories should not occur - after all there are frequent references, without details, to cures and miracles performed by Jesus - and why Matthew should choose to include only of them. On the other hand if Matthew were basing himself on Mark, his abridgement is poorly done. For in both Mark and Luke, after the demons have cried out with a loud voice, the author tells us that Jesus had ordered the unclean spirit out (Mk 5:8, Lk 8:29) before it had requested to be sent off into the pigs. But in Matthew's version Jesus' command is left out, which rather confuses the narrative. Now since Matthew's account is generally shorter, omitting, for example, the name 'Legion' given by Mark and Luke, another explanation seems as persuasive as mere muddle-headedness: Mark is not available at this point to Matthew. And of course Matthew does not have the Capernaum incident at all. Could the truth be not that Matthew has botched an amalgamation, but that *neither* section of Mark was before him? What about the fact that in Mark's version the demoniac's words are nearly identical on two different occasions? One thing that this does *not* prove is that only one incident is being described, for both incidents but only one set of dialogue may have been recorded in the tradition. Or the details of one incident may have been confused with those of another. It is easy to see why the stories of Capernaum and Gergesa could lead people to see a literary relationship between Mark and Luke; there is no good reason why such relationships should be posited here between Mark and Matthew.

7. **Peter's Mother-in-Law** (Mk 1:29 - 31, Mt 8:14 - 15, Lk 4:38 - 9)
It should merely be observed that Sanders has argued persuasively that
there is no common denominator in this section and that priority is impossible to determine.[73]

8 Preaching in Galilee (Mk 1:39, Mt 4:23, Lk 4:44)
In this section it is curious that whereas Matthew and Mark refer to 'their'
synagogues, Luke says 'synagogues of Judaea'. Literary relationship between Mark and Matthew looks possible, for this is a rather strange way of
speaking, perhaps indicating that the writers distinguished 'their' synagogues from 'ours'. This is a section where Matthew is fuller, as he continues to be in verse 24 where the odd reference to Syria suggests more than
mere editorializing. So Matthew expands Mark and has more than Mark
(but if so, why need it be Mark?) or, easier, Mark is a précis of Matthew,
which is possible but not necessary. Kilpatrick thought that 'their' synagogues dates from after the Birkath-ha-Minim, the benediction which made
it impossible for Christians to worship in synagogues.[74] But the peculiar
form merely suggests that the passages were composed where Judaism ver-
sus Jewish-Christianity was a real issue, i.e. in Palestine.[75]

9. **Healing a Leper** (Mk 1:40 - 5, Mt 8:1 - 4, Lk 5:12 - 16)
Mark and Luke present this story after the narrative of Jesus in Capernaum
and preaching in Galilee. In Matthew the preaching in Galilee is followed
by the Sermon on the Mount, but after the Sermon we revert, with the
healing of the leper, to the same sequence as Mark, though in the ensuing
pericopae divergences begin again. In other words we are now treating of
another of those sections where not only are the verbal parallels between
the three Synoptics very close, but their order also coincides. In the first
chapter I suggested that such material could be part of the simplest version
of a 'Gospel' narrative. In such sections it is particularly important to compare Matthew and Mark in detail.

Our present passage is thus a good example of the Triple Tradition, and
it is one in which, unlike the Preaching in Galilee which we have just discussed, Mark (and Luke) have more detail than Matthew. Examining it
more precisely, we find particularly close similarity in the words of the
leper and of Jesus ('If you wish, you can cleanse me' . . . 'I do wish; be
clean'). But there is much greater variation in the narrative itself, not significant for the meaning, but significant if literary derivation were involved.
In this case if Matthew has précised Mark he has done a very much better
job than he often does if we follow the précis theory. It is true that he
omits the graphic details ('And having sternly charged him
(ἐμβριμησάμενος),[76] he sent him away at once'), but he has avoided un-
clearness in so doing and also in his suppression of the fact (interesting if

perhaps editorial and repetitive) that the leper talked freely and attracted
a good deal of attention. At some stage we shall have to ask whether it is
more plausible that Matthew is capable of both good and incompetent
précis-work or that his versions of Markan material are not précis at all. In
such an enquiry it will be of importance if it turns out that the good work
occurs, as here, particularly in passages which we thought might be part of
a basic Gospel-outline or rudimentary account of the life of Jesus. For if
these passages were a homogeneous group, they would fall into the class of
material identified by Gaboury as 'set' or 'frozen' early in the development of the tradition. Thus it would not be surprising if Matthew's short
versions of such materials were unusually clear.

10.   Healing a Paralytic (Mk 2:1 - 12, Mt 9:1 - 8, Lk 5:17 - 26)
The treatment of this material in Matthew and Mark closely resembles
what we saw in the case of the leper. Mark's version is the more graphic,[77]
and many of its graphic details, such as the removal of the roof to bring
the paralytic to Jesus, recur in Luke. What Matthew preserves here is
largely the words of Jesus in a version very similar to Mark's with an ab-
solute minimum of surrounding narrative. The last lines of the story provide strange variants and are all that will be discussed here: Mark has 'They
were all amazed and glorified God, saying we never saw anything like this';
Luke gives 'Amazement seized them all and they glorified God and were
filled with awe, saying, "We have seen strange things today" '; Matthew,
however, is rather more diverse: 'They were afraid and they glorified God
who had given such authority to men'. Matthew's version refers to the
amazement of the crowd that authority had been given to Jesus. Thus he
seems to pick up Jesus' earlier words 'That you may know that the Son of
Man has authority to forgive sins'. But if so the text τοῖς ἀνθρώποις
is probably corrupt; as it stands it seems nearly meaningless. Perhaps
τῷ ἀνθρώπῳ was the original. But be that as it may, it *could* be argued
that at this point Matthew has produced a neater and more rounded ending
than Mark at the price of omitting what seem like the actual words spoken.
This might suggest that the ending in Matthew is a more worked-over version of a Markan original, but when coupled with the facts that this section
of Matthew is a clear short version, and that, as in the previous section, we
are dealing with a passage where both words and order are very close in all
three Synoptics, it might also raise the possibility that Matthew represents
one version of the tradition while Mark and Luke represent another.

11.   The Call of Levi/Matthew (Mt 9:9 - 13, Mk 2:13 - 17, Lk 5:27 - 32)
When discussing the call of the first disciples, we noted that Luke is clearly
following a different version, while Matthew and Mark are in a similar tradition, though it is impossible to determine whether either of them is

dependent on the other. But at 5:12 Luke reverts to the same tradition as the others (following Mark?), retelling the healing of the leper and the paralytic. In both these latter sections, as we have already noted, we may be dealing with a basic 'Gospel' account, and if so, that account also contained the next section, the call of Levi/Matthew, where again both wording and order bring all three Synoptics very close indeed. Now if we are here dealing not with Matthew and Luke copying Mark (though Luke probably is) but with at least Mark and Matthew following a primitive tradition, the question cannot but arise as to why the story of the call of Levi should belong to such a tradition, where the call of other disciples does not. Some might suppose that it is because the Synoptic tradition originated with Levi, and that the author of that tradition wished to identify himself as a very early follower of Jesus in order to provide guarantees of the authenticity of the material which he provides. This would lead to the theory that Levi/Matthew was some kind of quasi-official notetaker and that his position as such was recognized, and if there were other strong reasons to believe that Mark and Luke were dependent on Matthew or Proto-Matthew, we might accept this line of argument. If, however, it were to appear more likely that Mark and Matthew represent different versions of the basic tradition about Jesus, we should have to explain the inclusion of the call of Levi/Matthew in that tradition in some other way. And in fact a good explanation is ready to hand, an explanation that appeals not to the fact that it was Levi/Matthew who was called, but to the fact that the story deals with Jesus' appeal not to the 'righteous' (according to the Law), but to sinners. In other words to omit this story in any primitive account of Jesus' life and Passion would be to omit the Master's own explanation, or partial explanation, of the reason for his earthly career. In this connection it can be no accident that the call to publicans and sinners immediately precedes (in all three Synoptics) the question about fasting ('The Pharisees and the disciples of John fast, but your disciples do not'), and that the next section of all three Synoptics where words and order come together deals with plucking ears of grain on the Sabbath.

Turning again to details and looking for literary dependence, we notice *(a)* that Matthew speaks of 'Matthew' while Mark and Luke have 'Levi'[78] - a phenomenon which could be explained, but need not be, as Matthew 'adjusting' Mk 2:14 to bring it in line with 3:18;[79] and *(b)* that Matthew adds the words 'Go and learn what this means, "I desire mercy and not sacrifice" ' (Hosea 6:6). The words could easily be slipped in and may be out of sequence here; they occur again, for example, somewhat oddly at Mt 12:7. But if we are not faced with a mere floating 'particle', we may note that the words are missing in Mark and Luke. They may, of course, be editorializing. No further certainties or even likelihoods are available.

12.   The Question about Fasting (Mt 9:14 - 17, Mk 2:18 - 22, Lk 5:33 - 9) We are confronted here with a section dealing with Jesus' attitude to traditional strict observance,[80] as in the call of Levi, in which both words and position come together in all three Synoptics. As we have already suggested, such passages should be particularly important in determining possible literary dependence, for here, if anywhere, such dependence should be demonstrable. The pericope is joined somewhat roughly in both Mark and Matthew to the story of Levi; Luke, perhaps inadvertently, smooths the transition down, seemingly making the question 'Why do the disciples of John and of the Pharisees fast?' come, a little incongruously, from the Pharisees themselves. Mark agrees with Luke about the question referring both to the disciples of John and to those of the Pharisees, but makes no attempt to link it to the previous remarks of the Pharisees themselves, attributing it vaguely to people in general. Now Matthew, diverging from Mark and Luke, puts the question in the mouth of the disciples of John. It might be supposed that Matthew gets his version by a cursory (and faulty) reading of Mark: Mark reads καὶ ἦσαν οἱ μαθηταὶ Ἰωάννου καὶ οἱ Φαρισαῖοι νηστεύοντες, καὶ ἔρχονται   ... But if that was Matthew's procedure, it is very sloppy indeed, and it is curious that Matthew, normally so interested, it is said, in the Pharisees, should modify their role here. It is admittedly awkward to explain why Mark should *put in* the references to the Pharisees if he was following Matthew, but Matthew's sloppiness in abbreviating needs explanation too. This is not the only passage in which the price paid for the thesis that Matthew depends on Mark is the conviction of Matthew for incompetent work.

We have now reached the end of our discussion of the section we designated as a first testing ground for the literary hypothesis. We draw the following conclusions:

(i) Again and again it is impossible to determine from a comparison which Gospel depends on which.

(ii) Sometimes Matthew appears as a 'middle term' between Mark and Luke; more frequently Mark is a 'middle term' between Matthew and Luke; but being a middle term does not necessitate priority in regard to date of composition.

(iii) If we suppose that Matthew depends on Mark, we have to account for substantial differences in the quality of his abbreviating.

(iv) Difficulties in determining priorities are substantial in
Gaboury's section C, Gaboury's section D, passages which
might have the strongest claim to be part of the earliest form
of Christian preaching, and passages with perhaps less claims
to such primitivity. Difficulties are equally great in passages
where it might be supposed that Mark and Q overlap, and in
passages where no such desperate proposals have so far been
deemed necessary.

In view of these results we are justified in looking at further Synoptic
passages to see whether doubts about the literary hypothesis can be
confirmed.

3

VOCABULARY AND SEQUENCE: MATTHEW'S VERSION OF MK 2:23 - 6:13

If Matthew follows Mark and is concerned particularly about Mark's sequence, in section D as well as section C, as identified by Gaboury, then interlocking problems of sequence and vocabulary arise from his handling of Mk 2:23 - 6:13 (Mt 9:18 - 13:58). Let us begin by presenting the material in parallel columns, noting, as we have already, that leaving aside the Sermon on the Mount, there is a good deal of agreement in order (with a few additions and displacements) up to Mk 2:22 (Mt 9:17). From there we proceed as follows, observing that *the parallels are only approximate:*

Mk	Mt	Lk
2:22	9:17	-
2:23 - 38	12:1 - 8	6:1 - 5
3:1 - 6	12:9 - 14	6:6 - 11
3:7 - 12	12:15 - 21	6:17 - 19
3:13 - 19	10:1 - 4	6:12 - 16
		'Sermon on the Plain', etc. (6:20 - 8:3)
3:20 - 2	12:22 - 4	11:14 - 16
3:23 - 30	12:25 - 37	11:17 - 23
-	12:38 - 42	11:29 - 32
-	12:43 - 5	11:24 - 6
3:31 - 5	12:46 - 50	8:19 - 21
4:1 - 9	13:1 - 9	8:4 - 8
4:10 - 12 (omits Mt 13:12 after 4:11)	13:10 - 15	8:9 - 10
4:13 - 20	13:18 - 23	8:11 - 15
4:21 - 4	-	8:16 - 18a
4:25	(13:12)	8:18b
4:26 - 9	-	-
-	13:24 - 30	-

Mk	Mt	Lk
4:30 - 2	13:31 - 2	13:18 - 19
-	13:33	13:20 - 1
4:33 - 4	13:34 - 5	-
-	13:36 - 43	-
-	13:44 - 6	-
-	13:47 - 50	-
-	13:51 - 2	-
(3:31 - 5)	12:46 - 50	8:19 - 21
4:35 - 41	-	8:22 - 5
5:1 - 20	-	8:26 - 39
5:21 - 43	-	8:40 - 56
6:1 - 6a	13:53 - 8	-

A great variety of problems becomes evident when the material is set out in this form. They include the following:

1.

Where, if anywhere, do we find the Markan parallels to Mt 10:1 - 11:30? We notice that both Matthew and Luke leave Markan sequence at the same place, viz. 3:19. At this point Luke starts on his 'Sermon on the Plain', which may be left aside. The question which we are interested in is why Luke moves away from Mark's sequence at precisely the same point as Matthew. It is obviously not because he is following Matthew's narrative; it must be because he thinks that Markan order is not the only possible order at this point in the traditional accounts, the point, that is, where Jesus chooses the Twelve.

Let us now inspect the Markan order, where possible, for the events listed in Matthew 10:1 - 11:30:

Mt	Mk	(Lk)	
10:1 - 4	3:13 - 19	6:12 - 16	Choosing the Twelve
10:5 - 15	6:7 - 13	9:1 - 6	Sending out of Twelve (in Markan order)
10:16		10:4	But Luke deals with the 70

Mt	Mk	(Lk)	
10:17 - 21 (cf.			
24:9 - 12)	13: 9 - 12	21:12 - 16 ⌉	
10:22 (cf.			
24:12b - 13)	13:13	21:17 - 19	
10:23	-	-	Fate of Disciples
10:24 - 5a	-	6:40	
10:25b	-	- ⌋	
10:26	4:22	8:17	
10:26 - 33	-	12:2 - 9	Exhortation to speak out boldly
10:34 - 6	-	12:51 - 3	Division in households
10:37 - 9 (cf.			
16:24 - 5)	- (cf. 8:34 - 5)	14:26 - 7	(cf. 9:23 - 4)
10:40 (cf.			
18:5)	- (cf. 9:37)	-	(cf. 9:48) ⌉
10:41	-	-	End of discourse
10:42	9:41	-	
11:1	-	- ⌋	
11:2 - 6	-	7:18 - 23	John's Question to Jesus
11:7 - 19	-	7:24 - 35	Jesus on John
11:20 - 4	-	10:13 - 15	Woes on Galilee
11:25 - 7	-	10:21 - 2	Thanksgiving of Jesus
11:28 - 30	-	-	Comfort for heavy-laden

It appears from our earlier collocation of passages that if Matthew is following Mark, Matthew 10:1 - 4 is in the wrong place. Matthew 10:1 - 4 should in fact appear at 12:22ff., if Matthew were following Mark at this point, for Mt 10:1 looks parallel to Mk 3:13. But, of course, Matthew has written 10:1 - 4 at an earlier stage of the narrative. Our query as to what Matthew was doing when he reached 10:1 is clarified by the following passages:

Mt	Mk	Lk	
9:18 - 26	5:21 - 43	8:40 - 56	Jairus' daughter
9:27 - 31	10:46 - 52	18:35 - 43	Two blind men
9:32 - 4 (cf. 12:22 - 4)	-	(cf. 11:14 -	
		15)	Dumb demoniac
9:35 (cf. 4:23)	-	-	
9:36	6:34	-	
9:37 - 8	-	10:2	Sending out
			disciples
10:1	-	-	

It is clear from this that throughout the latter part of chapter 9 Matthew
is not following Mark (even where he preserves material also to be found in
Mark). But at 10:1 he might seem to pick up the Markan material, however
briefly. Let us compare Mt 10:1 with Mk 3:13. If Matthew had been following Mark at this point, he could not have failed to realize that Mark is
describing the appointment of twelve specially chosen men as apostles. But
Matthew's version muddles this up. He begins, 'And having summoned his
twelve apostles'; there is nothing about a special selection and commission.
Luke is much closer to Mark and gets the sense right; 'He called his disciples and chose from them twelve' (6:13). The conclusion is that Matthew
cannot have been following Mark 3 when he wrote 10:1 (and it is highly
unlikely that Mark 3 was following Matthew either, for he has brought order
into Matthew's chaos and completely scrapped the Matthaean order). The
implication of this passage is that Mark and Matthew, in reproducing similar
material, are quite independent of each other. The defence that Mt 10:1 is
a vague 'memory' of Mark is made more unlikely by the non-Markan context in which it appears. In fact 10:1 is an 'echo', or more likely a parallel
version, of Mk 6:7 (=Lk 9:1).

2.

Assuming that Matthew is not reverting to Mark, even for sequence, when
he pens 10:1, what do we find happening when he reaches 12:21? Does
he start following Mark there? Of course, 12:17 - 21 are not in Mark at all;
indeed they have no parallel in the Synoptics. And the previous verses
(12:15 - 16), though vaguely parallel to Mk 3:7 - 12, are the merest skeleton
of the Markan version. It is true that they *could* be a reduction of Mark,
but it is more likely that they derive from another source, for it would then
follow that verses 17 - 21, the prophecy from Isaiah, derive from that same
other source; they certainly must come from somewhere.

But what of Mt 12:1 - 14? This section breaks into two parts, Plucking
Ears of Grain on the Sabbath (verses 1 - 8) and Healing the Man with the

Withered Hand (verses 9 - 14). These are both in the Triple Tradition, and it may be thought that Matthew, who abandons Markan order at 9:17 to give us a good deal of material some of which occurs elsewhere in Mark, returns to it, as does Luke, at 12:1. Thus Matthew would here be following the 'normal' Lucan pattern of inserting a block of non-Markan material into Markan sequence.

Now we shall see that Matthew is not following Mark in chapter 11, and we have already observed that Mt 12:15ff. is probably not derived from Mark; so on the 'Markan' hypothesis 12:1 - 14 would be a brief 'Markan' insert in a long non-Markan section. That is possible, but rather implausible. It would be much simpler to argue that the whole section of Matthew from 9:17 to 12:37 and beyond derives from a source other than Mark.

But let us also look at 12:1 - 14. The first part of this is one of the 'basic Gospel' sections we have already observed. In Mark it follows immediately on a similar section we discussed in Chapter Two, namely the Question about Fasting. Now we have the question about Sabbath observance. It might be supposed that Mark is here following basic Christian preaching in presenting material as he does; certainly Mk 2:23, though having connections in thought with 2:22, does not follow in any necessary chronological sequence. Luke's order is exactly Mark's in these sections, compelling us to take direct dependence seriously, though there are minor variations of wording and some omissions (e.g. 'when Abiathar was high-priest') which correspond with Matthew. Matthew's narrative, viewed in relation to Mark's, is striking: verses 1 - 4 are very close with little 'compression' or 'expansion'; 5 - 7 are non-Markan (indeed put in only because a *similar* topic is involved); 8 is abbreviated; 9 - 10 are more or less parallel though Mark continues with a section Matthew omits (3:3=Lk 6:8); 11 is absent from Mark; 12 is abbreviated; 13 is more or less parallel but omits to mention the Herodians.[81] What can be deduced from this? Clearly Matthew could depend on Mark, but if so, his approach to him fluctuates greatly within a very short space, now expanding, now more or less repeating, now contracting. At the least Matthew has to use Q as well as Mark, but Two-Documentarians, of course, would approve of that; and were this passage surrounded by material where Matthew is obviously following Mark, one might have no hesitation about it. But if it is not so surrounded, it might be more plausible to suppose that literary dependence is not the answer, for it certainly need not be. And to abandon literary dependence is to dissolve the difficulty of explaining why within so short a compass Matthew is able to react so differently to the Markan version.

Let us return to Matthew 12:22. The parallel to this would need to be at Mk 3:20 if Matthew were following the order found in Mark at this point. But of course the actual Mk 3:20 - 1 is missing in Matthew, and the healing in Mt 12:22ff. does not occur in Mark. So Mk 3:20 - 1 is added to Matthew if Mark is using Matthew, and Matthew's healing, not derived from Mark, must come from Q at best.[82] In fact the Matthew healing is a doublet; something similar also occurred at 9:32 - 4, as our previous table showed. But Mark does not have this passage either, so once again Matthew did not copy Mark, and obviously Mark did not copy Matthew. It looks as though Matthew knew two versions of this story, but neither of them came from Mark, and on a Q hypothesis it is hard to see which one of them has more claim to be regarded as Q. So we have to conclude that, although (e.g.) Mt 12:24 (the follow-up to the demoniacs) occurs in the Triple Tradition, there is no justification for claiming that Matthew took this passage from Mark, even though the language now becomes very close to Mark's, for he probably had at least two other versions available. The caution may perhaps be axiomatized: it is rash to *assume* that very similar wording has anything to do with the direct use of one Gospel by the author of another. Other passages will tend to confirm the importance of this axiom.

3.

We have argued that Mt 12:15 - 24, although in parts containing parallel material to Mark, should not be derived directly from Mark. If we proceed to the section Mt 12:25 - 37, we find a similar situation. In much of this section Luke is closer to Matthew than to Mark; and sometimes Matthew, sometimes Mark, gives the fuller version. These features are particularly interesting and we should note them carefully in view of the fact that we are dealing for much of this section with similar material in all three Synoptics, yet in a passage where Mark and Matthew seem to be parallel but distinct. The fact is that there are often close verbal similarities between Mark and Matthew which we should not now wish necessarily to attribute to a literary relationship. Compare, for example, Mt 12:29 with Mk 3:27.

The second point to be noticed is that while Mark in verse 28 says that sins will be forgiven the sons of men, Matthew (cf. Lk 12:10) speaks of men's sins being forgiven and adds that this includes speaking against the Son of Man. There may well be a confusion in the 'original' saying here, but the two texts cannot be the product of direct literary dependence unless, once again, astonishing carelessness is shown by someone. Again, possibly, we may be dealing with a 'memory' rather than with a check by Mark of Matthew or Matthew of Mark, but why is that necessary? If we are to invoke 'memory', there were probably many 'traditions' available. Why assume, merely because we have the texts of Mark and Matthew, that it is one of these two texts that is being remembered?[83]

4.

Let us now proceed to Mt 12:38ff., the refusal of Jesus to provide a sign.
At this point we are in a non-Markan passage, or, as more would say, a Q
passage, for there is a clear parallel with Luke 11:29ff. Now, although the
passages in Matthew and Luke are parallel, they do not occur in the same
place in the narrative, as is common enough for such 'non-Markan' material. Luke 11 in fact is part of Luke's special 'Travel Narrative'. However Matthew also has a very similar section elsewhere, this time in a
Markan context and with a parallel in Mark (but not in Luke). Both
Matthew and Mark place this section after the Feeding of the 4000
(Mt 16:1, 2, 4 = Mk 8:11 - 13). What conclusions should be drawn from
this? At first sight it would seem the obvious approach to say that Matthew
'found' his 12:38 - 42 passage in Q, as did Luke, and then, finding it again
in Mark, reproduced the same story in chapter 16. But difficulties about
this 'obvious' interpretation appear as soon as we begin to inspect Mt 16.
First of all it is not Mt 16, but Mt 12, which in its opening sentences looks
more like Mk 8 in the following ways:

  (i) Mt 12 and Mk 8 have no mention of Sadducees, in whom
      Matthew is rather interested, as we have already indicated.
      Mt 16 mentions the Sadducees.
 (ii) Mt 12 and Mk 8 proceed directly from the Pharisees' request
      for a sign from heaven to the reply that no sign shall be given,
      though there are differences in detail here. Mt 16, on the other
      hand, adds in most of verse 2 and all of verse 3 about inter-
      preting redness in the sky, material which admittedly appears
      in Luke, but in quite another context.

Thus the conclusion that should be drawn about Mt 16:1ff. and
Mk 8:11ff. is not that Matthew follows Mark (and perhaps blends him with
something else), nor that Mark follows Matthew, for he adds in details such
as 'He sighed deeply in his spirit', but that although Matthew 16:1 is in the
same position as Mark's parallel passage, Matthew does not draw this section from Mark. But, it will be said, surely Matthew has assimilated non-
Markan material into a Markan account. Again no-one can deny this is
possible; the question rather is how likely it is to be correct. Doubtless
the addition of the Sadducees can be explained away 'easily' enough, but
the ends of the two passages are significantly different. Where Mark has
'No sign shall be given to this generation', Matthew has the more explicit,
'No sign shall be given except the sign of Jonah' (which is already available). We must certainly allow again the possibility that Matthew knows
two traditions of this incident - unless, of course, there were two similar

incidents, and that is not impossible - but that neither tradition, despite first appearances, derives from Mark. And there is no reason to think the converse either, that Mark derives from Matthew, for if he had taken Matthew's story at 16:1 in the place where he found it, it is hard to see why he has embroidered it so as to make a substantive change.

5.

Our next text must be the Parable of the Sower (Mk 4:1 - 9, Mt 13:1 - 9, Lk 8:4 - 8). The texts are more or less parallel in all three Synoptics, and much of them would have to be included, as we have seen, in 'basic Gospel' material. Direct literary derivation might seem plausible, for problems of sequence are less in evidence than in some of the passages we have just considered, and direct verbal dependence looks likely. But let us look closer. Mark introduces the parable in what has been recognized as a somewhat odd fashion: he writes, 'He taught them many things in parables, and in his teaching (ἐν τῇ διδαχῇ αὐτοῦ) he said to them', etc. We should expect several parables at this point, but he only gives us one before Jesus goes on to provide his reason for speaking in parables. True, more parables follow eventually (Mk 4:26ff.), but the original plural of Mk 4:2 (repeated at 4:10) is a little clumsy, and was evidently thought strange by Luke (if he follows Mark), for he replaces the plural by a singular. More striking, however, is the phrase 'in his teaching' which Mark gives and which both Matthew and Luke omit. Certainly the phrase seems clumsy and unnecessary in Mark, unless, perhaps, we have some reference to what was recognized by Mark himself as a body of teaching material somehow existing in the Church and on which Mark indicates he is drawing at this point.[84] One of the phenomena which we have noticed already is that there seems to be evidence of verbal agreements between Mark and Matthew even in passages where literary derivation is unlikely. That in turn points to a 'source' of some kind available to both Mark and Matthew, and we have already noted more than once that verbal agreement is particularly likely to occur in texts recording the words of Jesus or questions put to him. Could such material be what Mark refers to as 'the teaching'? Possibly, but it seems most unlikely to be Matthew's Gospel or any vaguely equivalent earlier version of it.

There is a second passage of Mark (again not reproduced by Matthew or Luke) where the phrase 'in his teaching' occurs, namely 12:38, a section containing polemic against the scribes. Now the section 12:38 - 40, set in the Temple, looks a little out of place in Mark. True, Mark has been describing Jesus' dealings with the scribes in the Temple, and has just been discussing the scribal saying that Christ is the son of David, but it is just an anti-scribal context which seems to have given Mark the opportunity to insert our passage from 'the teaching'. It may even be that Mark is indicating a source at this point which is different from his source of the rest of the Temple narrative. In fact Mark's polemic against the scribes is a pale version of what we find in Matthew, where not just the scribes are attacked, but, in great detail, the scribes and the Pharisees. Luke follows Mark at this point, but it is hard to see how Mark is following Matthew's far more vivid narrative.[85] It is as near certain as anything can be in Synoptic criticism that, although Mark and Matthew are in the same sequence here, Mark is not following Matthew, while Matthew is deriving most, and most probably all, of his material from some source other than Mark. Mark's source may well be some particular document or tradition that he describes as 'the teaching', but there is no reason to suppose that Matthew's source is identical. (And we should notice, for good measure, that although Luke knows some parts of the long denunciation of the Pharisees that follows in Matthew, he by no means knows it all; there is no reason to suppose that it is precisely Matthew whom Luke is following at this point. Luke and Matthew probably have independent, but parallel sources for this section.)

Let us now see how this phenomenon of 'the teaching', observed again in Mk 12:38, can be investigated in Mk 4:1ff., the Parable of the Sower. Fortunately we have another version of this parable, in addition to the three Synoptics, namely that of the Gospel of Thomas (*logion* 9).[86] Let us look at the following parallels:

Mt	Mk	Lk	Ts[87]
Some seed fell along the road (ὁδός),[88]	Some seed fell along the road (ὁδός),	Some fell along the road (ὁδός) *and was trodden down,*	Some fell *on* the road,
and the birds came and devoured them.	and the birds came and devoured it.	and the birds of the air devoured it.	The birds came, they *gathered* them.
Other seeds fell on rocky ground, where they had not much soil, and immediately they sprang up, since they had no depth of	Other seed fell on rocky ground, where it had not much soil, and immediately it sprang up, since it had no depth of	And some fell on the rock (πέτρα), and as it grew up, it withered away, because it had no	Other fell on the rock (πέτρα) and it did not strike

soil, but when the sun rose they were scorched, and since they had no root they withered away.	soil; but when the sun rose it was scorched, and since it had no root it withered away.		moisture (ἰκμάδα)[89] root in the earth *and did not produce ears.*
Other seeds fell upon thorns, and the thorns grew up and choked them.	Other seed fell among thorns and the thorns grew up and choked it, *and it yielded no grain.*	And some fell among thorns; and the thorns grew with it and choked it.	And others fell in the thorns; they choked the seed *and the worm ate them.*
Other seeds fell on good soil, and brought forth fruit, some a hundred-fold, some sixty, some thirty.	And other seeds fell into good soil and brought forth fruit, *growing-up and increasing* and yielding thirty-fold and sixty-fold and a hundred-fold	And some fell into good soil and grew and yielded a hundred-fold	And others fell on the good earth; and it brought forth good fruit (καρπός); it bore 60 per measure and *120* per measure.

Now it is probably to be accepted that the Gospel of Thomas in its present form is a second-century document, that is, that it is later than any of our Synoptics. And we may also accept as likely that its author knew some, and perhaps indeed all, of the Synoptic Gospels when he compiled his own material. But in the Parable of the Sower, there is a certain amount of material in Thomas which the other Synoptics do not have. Some of this, of course, may be the invention of the author (or of his predecessors), but where the author has little apparent motive for such invention we have to face the possibility of an original tradition, independent of the Synoptics. Such additional variants as 'they gathered them', 'and the worm ate them', '120 per measure' seem to spring from no Gnostic or otherwise theological axe-grinding, and may well point to some independent tradition. There is a certain amount of evidence that elsewhere Thomas has access to such traditions, and he may well have it here also. If so, this tradition might bear some relation to the 'teaching' to which Mark refers. At the very least we may conclude that Thomas' version of this parallel tends to support, rather than to damage, our thesis about the nature of the sources of Mark and

Matthew. In particular it may reinforce the opinion that it is simplistic to equate 'the teaching' with Matthew or the source of Matthew.

6.

After giving us the Parable of the Sower, all the Synoptics proceed to the notoriously difficult explanation of the purpose of parables. The comparative sequence in the three Gospels is as follows for this and succeeding sections:

Mt		Mk		Lk
13:10 - 11	=	4:10 - 11	=	8:9 - 10
13:12	=	(4:25 - 6)	=	(8:18)
13:13		4:12		8:10
13:14 - 15		-		-
13:16 - 17		-		10:23 - 4
13:18 - 23		4:13 - 20		8:11 - 15
(13:12)		4:21 - 5		8:16 - 18

Our interest in this passage is not in the variations of order between Mark and Matthew, which are slight. Indeed the section might look like a good example of Matthew combining Mark with Q. And it is readily apparent that Luke 8:9 - 18 follows a Markan order; I should say that Luke almost certainly has Mark available to him at this point. My interest, rather, is in the well-known crux about the Purpose of Speaking in Parables in Mk 4:12 and parallels. Here Mark, followed by Luke, writes as follows: '*so that* they may indeed see but not perceive and may indeed hear but not understand'. Luke leaves out Mark's final line 'Lest they should turn again and be forgiven'. Matthew, however, reads not 'so that' ($\H{\iota} \nu \alpha$), but 'because' ($\H{o} \tau \iota$), thus producing a far gentler sense,[90] but one that is not easy to square with the text of Isaiah, to which, in contrast to Mark and Luke, he specifically refers. A common explanation offered is that Matthew, faced with a text he cannot stomach in Mark, has watered it down;[91] Luke, however, has preserved the original Markan sense. Those who have looked at the Gospels in the hope of identifying an original Aramaic tradition have made much play with this passage. Both $\H{o} \tau \iota$ (Mt) and $\H{\iota} \nu \alpha$ (Mk, Lk) must, they say, be translations (or adaptations) of the same original d[e] particle in Aramaic.[92] Thus if the original deposit of tradition in Aramaic gave that particle, both Matthew's and Mark's versions are linguistically possible. There is, of course, a persistent tradition in antiquity that Matthew's Gospel was originally written in 'the Hebrew dialect' (Aramaic?), and we shall return to this at a later stage. For the moment we should note that *if* the original Matthew was Aramaic, then both our Matthew and our Mark *could* derive from it, one being a free rendering and the other using Aramaic Matthew as its literary source. Obviously, however, the possible existence at this point of the tradition of the Aramaic d^e particle does not demand that Mark used an Aramaic Matthew. On the other hand if this particle existed behind Mark it might point to the fact that he did not use our Matthew at this point in his narrative. Beyond that linguistic arguments will not take us, and we cannot even be certain that the explanation of the divergences between Mark and Matthew in terms of the d^e particle is correct.

Mark 4:21 is missing in Matthew, but occurs in Luke (8:16). Luke also has a second related passage at 11:33ff. It is interesting to analyse Luke's text in the two passages and see what light this analysis sheds on the relation between Matthew and Mark. Let us begin with Lk 11:33 - 6. We find here a pattern of parallel passages in Matthew as follows:

Mt	Lk
5:15	11:33
6:22 - 3	11:34 - 5
	11:36

It is generally recognized that Luke is inclined to assemble material from each of his separate sources in blocks while Matthew is more inclined to split it up. This may well be the case here. Matthew has in fact put material he 'found' in the same source as Luke in different parts of his Sermon on the Mount, while Luke has kept it together in his 'Travel Narrative'. Now both Luke 11:29 - 32 (Asking for a Sign) and 11:33 - 6 (Light under a Bushel) appear in Matthew, but in different places, and we should probably infer from this *either* that Luke's source contained these two sections together, or that Luke changes sources after verse 32. Now Luke's source in 11:33 is certainly not Mark, for he seems to have followed Mark for the same material earlier, at 8:16. So if Luke is following the same non-Markan source for both 11:29 - 32 and 11:33, then if Mt 5:15 parallels Lk 11:33, the source of Mt 5:15 is presumably not Mark either. And the same follows for Mt 5:15 if Lk 11:29 - 32 and 11:33 follow different but similar non-Markan sources. Thus if Mt 5:15 parallels Lk 11:33 rather than Mk 4:21 - 5 (=Lk 8:16 - 18), we have to conclude that, although Mark has the lamp under the bushel story, Matthew does not get his version of that story from Mark. Let us look at the four relevant passages:

Mt 5:15 οὐδὲ καίουσιν λύχνον καὶ τιθέασιν αὐτὸν ὑπὸ τὸν
μόδιον ἀλλ᾽ἐπὶ τὴν λυχνίαν, καὶ λάμπει πᾶσιν
τοῖς ἐν τῇ οἰκίᾳ.

Mk 4:21 μήτι ἔρχεται ὁ λύχνος ἵνα ὑπὸ τὸν μόδιον τεθῇ ἢ
ὑπὸ τὴν κλίνην· οὐχ ἵνα ἐπὶ τὴν λυχνίαν τεθῇ;

Lk 8:16 Οὐδεὶς δὲ λύχνον ἅψας καλύπτει αὐτὸν σκεύει ἢ
ὑποκάτω κλίνης τίθησιν, ἀλλ᾽ἐπὶ λυχνίας τίθησιν,
ἵνα οἱ εἰσπορευόμενοι βλέπωσιν τὸ φῶς.

Lk 11:33 Οὐδεὶς λύχνον ἅψας εἰς κρύπτην τίθησιν [οὐδὲ ὑπὸ
τὸν μόδιον] ἀλλ᾽ἐπὶ τὴν λυχνίαν, ἵνα οἱ εἰσπορευόμενοι
τὸ φῶς βλέπωσιν

Looking at these four texts can we see the relationship between them, and
in particular can we determine anything about the source of Matthew?
The chief differences between Matthew and Mark are twofold - and in connection with this we must recognize that Matthew is *not* following a
Markan order at this point:

(i) Matthew has nothing about a bed (though Luke 8:16, in
Markan order, has).
(ii) Mark has nothing about illuminating people in the house.

In other words it is hard to argue either that Mark has compressed Matthew
or that Matthew has compressed Mark. Nor, of course, can it be said that
Matthew has consistently expanded Mark, for he omits some Markan material. It must probably also be admitted that Luke, although following
a 'Markan' framework at this point, does not follow Mark's narrative as
his primary source (or perhaps even as his source at all). On the other hand
both Lucan passages have similarities with Matthew. Since, however, it
seems that Luke 8:16, though 'Markan' in framework, is not verbally derived primarily from Mark, this need not disturb us. The source of Mt 5:15
is not Mark, even though the material does appear in some guise in Mark.
Thus in this passage we conclude that if Matthew does have Mark, he dis-
regards the Markan text in favour of another authority. More likely, perhaps, he does not have Mark?

7.

It is now time to go back to the collection of non-Markan material in chapters 10 and 11 of Matthew. We agreed at an earlier stage that it is very unlikely that Matthew is following Mark 3 at 10:1. It is now time to enquire
in a little more detail into what happens in the remaining parts of this un-

Markan section of Matthew, beginning with the observation, clear from our table on pp. 35 - 6, that Matthew does not follow Mark's order here and that Luke clearly does not follow Matthew's order. Certainly there are parallels between Matthew and Luke, but they are not particularly protracted. In other words Luke does not use at least any very extended blocks of material drawn either from Matthew or from Matthew's source if Matthew represents the order of that source.

(a) The list of apostles (Mt 10:2 - 4, Mk 3:16 - 19 Lk 6:13 - 16 (cf. Acts 1:13))

In both Mark and Luke the list of apostles is in its obvious place, that is, just after Jesus had identified twelve individuals from all his followers as apostles. In Matthew, since, as we have seen, there is no clear parallel to the Call, the list is inserted in a rather different way. Obviously Matthew wants to name the Twelve, and he takes the opportunity to do so at the point in his narrative when he wishes to describe the preaching mission by the disciples which Jesus himself initiated. Of the list of apostles itself little need be said here. None of the lists is in exactly the same order, and where Matthew and Mark have Thaddaeus, Luke (and Acts) have Judas the son of James, who may or may not be a different person; but nothing can be drawn from any of this about the primitivity of any of the versions we have.

(b) The Mission in Matthew (10:5ff.)

The next section of chapter 10, however, provides a great deal of interesting information. In the first place Matthew gives a specific account of a mission designed for Jews only. Not only Gentiles but Samaritans also are excluded. This section (10:5 - 8) has no parallel in Mark or Luke, but Matthew reaches 'Markan - Lucan' material in verse 9, which has its parallels right at the end of Gaboury's 'less formed' section D, that is, just before all three Synoptics move to their description of Herod thinking that Jesus is John the Baptist risen from the dead. We shall look at the strange presentation of this material in Matthew at a later stage; for the time being we merely note that not only does Matthew not follow the order of Mark and Luke in his passage about the sending out of the Twelve, but his material is different, in particular, as we have seen, in that it contains a passage dealing explicitly with a mission to the Jews only. It is sometimes suggested or implied that this 'national-minded command' is the product of a later split within the Christian community between Judaizers and the followers of Paul - a possible but by no means necessary explanation. In fact nothing is more likely than that Jesus did originally wish to restrict his mission to Jews; certainly it would have required a good deal of instruction to be given to his disciples before they could comprehend anything else. The point is also made clear by implication in the stories of the centurion's servant (Mt 8:5 - 13, Lk 7:1 - 10) - particularly in Luke's version where the elders of the Jews explain to Jesus how benevolent the man had been to Judaism - and of the Canaanite ('Syrophoenician') woman (Mt 15:21 - 8, Mk 7:24 - 30). It should probably be deduced from these accounts that Jesus' own comprehension of his mission developed as he proceeded. If that is so, then the 'Jewish' material in the Sending Out passage of Matthew probably indicates something primitive, rather than something developed, or interpolated; or at least that it is as likely to do so. And there is no reason why Matthew should not have the material (not used by Mark and Luke) in its right place; certainly the place where he inserts it is curiously appropriate.

We have already noticed that Mt 10:1 - 4 finds its closest parallel in the sixth chapter of Mark, though the context is different. The parallel continues when we reach verse 9 of chapter 10, which is parallel, but not particularly closely parallel, to Mk 6:8ff. and Lk 10:4ff. All three texts are interlocking, and direct literary dependence of any of them on any other is not self-evident. Sometimes, it must be said, however, Luke appears to be a consolidation of Markan and Matthaean material. When we read Mt 10:17, though, a different, though related problem arises. Mt 10:17ff. is closely related to material which appears elsewhere in Matthew in a position common to all three Synoptics, that is, to material which occurs in the so-called Synoptic Apocalypse (Mt 24:9ff., Mk 13:9ff., Lk 21:12ff.).

Let us examine Mt 10:17ff. verse by verse. In doing so, we shall be forced to the realization that Matthew gets some comparable material from two separate traditions, neither of which he is willing to abandon entirely:

Mt 10:17 - 18　　　Both Mark and Luke include this material in the Synoptic Apocalypse, where it seems more appropriate, for at Mt 10:17 there is little likelihood that the disciples will shortly be dragged before governors and kings. Indeed the reference to the Gentiles in Mt 10:17 bears this out, and in the parallel passage of Mark (13:10) we actually find a text contrary in spirit to Mt 10:5 - 6, namely 'The gospel must first be preached to all nations'. This phrase occurs rightly in Matthew at 24:14.

Mt 10:19 - 21　　　This appears as Mk 13:11 - 12, Lk 21:14 - 16.

Mt 10:22a   'And you will be hated by all for my name's sake'.
Compare Mt 24:9b 'and you will be hated by all
nations for my name's sake', Mk 13:13 'and you will be
hated by all for my name's sake', and Lk 21:17 'you
will be hated by all for my name's sake'.

We notice that, although the two Matthew passages are similar, yet the first
one, omitting 'nations', is more appropriate to a Jewish situation. At any
rate the basic issues are clear: Matthew has two sets of material describing
the difficulties the disciples will face, one dealing with a mission only
within Israel, ('You will not have gone through all the towns of Israel, before the Son of Man comes'), the other in a wider context. But there is
no reason why these two sets may not represent different utterances of
Jesus in different contexts, as Matthew, but not Mark and Luke, suggests.[93]
The indications are, therefore, that Matthew may well preserve the primitive account of the development of Jesus' concept of his mission, or of the
different stages in which he envisioned carrying out that mission.

(c) Lights and bushels
At Mt 10:26 we read as follows: 'So have no fear of them; for nothing is
covered that will not be revealed, or hidden that will not be known'. This
section, and what follows, appears in Luke (12:2ff.) in a slightly expanded
version. More interestingly it appears again in the same context in Mark
and Luke in the discussion of the purpose of parables (Mk 4:22, Lk 8:16).
Which context is the original? Or are both genuine? For we must not forget the possibility that many of the sayings of Jesus were uttered on several different occasions, each thus being a source for a different 'tradition'.
The context of Mt 10:26 is certainly appropriate, though, of course, it
does not follow from that that this is the original location of the saying,
for Matthew could well have inserted it here, even if he did know, or remember, the original context, simply because it is appropriate. But Mk
4:22 (Lk 8:17) seems less appropriate. By the end of Mk 4:20 the author
has completed his interpretation of the Parable of the Sower. He then
proceeds as follows (with Luke following the same pattern, though, as we
have seen, probably not under the primary influence of Mark): 'And he
said to them, "Is a lamp brought in to be put under a bushel, or under a
bed and not on a stand?" For there is nothing hid except to be made mani-
fest; nor is anything secret, except to come to light. If any man has ears
to hear, let him hear', etc. Certainly it seems reasonable enough for Mark
(and Luke) to put 'For there is nothing hid' after the lamp and the bushel,
and it may well be that these two sayings were originally uttered together.
But neither follows particularly well after the interpretation of the Sower.

Indeed it might seem more appropriate to carry on directly from Mk 4:20
to Mk 4:26, the parable of the Seed Growing Secretly. But Mark must
have had some reason for inserting the verses where he did - even though it
is hard for us to discover at this stage what that reason was. One thing,
however, is clear: Mark did *not* put this material where he did because he
was following Matthew, for, as we have seen, Matthew does not record it
in this context. It might, presumably, be argued that Mark found it in
Matthew 5:15 and shifted it here, but that suggestion lacks plausibility unless a good reason can be found why Mark should blend Mt 5:15 and 10:26
and then insert both of them together here. Of course, if our earlier
argument is correct, viz. that in this passage Luke, though possessed of
Markan material, is primarily following a source other than Mark, we might
surmise that Mark put the material here because he knew (but not of course
from Matthew) that this was one place where it was traditionally put. But
we have to revert to our earlier point: at least as regards Mk 4:22/Mt 10:26,
Matthew seems to have the more appropriate context from the point of
view of the continuity of the narrative.

(d) Conditions of discipleship
Mt 10:37 - 8 indicates the terms or conditions under which one must live
to be a disciple. This is a Q passage; its Lucan parallel is 14:26 - 7, though
there are interesting variants in the texts of Matthew and Luke. The next
verse in Matthew does not occur in the same place in Luke; rather it appears at Lk 17:33. More interesting, however, is that verses 38 - 9 of
Matthew (27 of Luke) reappear in the Triple Tradition, with a parallel passage in Mark: Mt 16:24b - 25, Mk 8:34b - 35, Lk 9:23 - 4. Let us look at
the two versions of Matthew and Luke first.

Mt 10:38 - 9   καὶ ὃς οὐ λαμβάνει τὸν σταυρὸν αὐτοῦ καὶ ἀκολουθεῖ
                ὀπίσω μου, οὐκ ἐστιν μου ἄξιος. ὁ εὑρὼν τὴν ψυχὴν
                αὐτοῦ ἀπολέσει αὐτήν, καὶ ὁ ἀπολέσας τὴν ψυχὴν
                αὐτοῦ ἕνεκεν ἐμοῦ εὑρήσει αὐτήν.

Mt 16:24b - 25 Εἴ τις θέλει ὀπίσω μου ἐλθεῖν, ἀπαρνησάσθω
                ἑαυτὸν καὶ ἀράτω τὸν σταυρὸν αὐτοῦ καὶ ἀκολουθείτω
                μοι. ὃς γὰρ ἐὰν θέλη τὴν ψυχὴν αὐτοῦ σῶσαι
                ἀπολέσει αὐτήν· ὃς δ᾽ ἂν ἀπολέσῃ τὴν ψυχὴν
                αὐτοῦ ἕνεκεν ἐμοῦ εὑρήσει αὐτήν.

It seems fairly clear that these are basically two versions of the same
tradition. The first version is preceded by the lines about loving Jesus
more than father and mother; the second assumes something of the same
kind in the phrase 'deny himself' which, as we shall see, reminds us of the

Lk 14 version of this incident. Yet the two versions are also significantly different verbally, or at least suggest that Matthew obtained them from different sources. That would account for their appearing in different places in his narrative.

Turning now to Luke, we read as follows:

Lk 14:27 ὅστις οὐ βαστάζει τὸν σταυρὸν ἑαυτοῦ καὶ ἔρχεται
ὀπίσω μου οὐ δύναται εἶναί μου μαθητής

Lk 9:23 Εἴ τις θέλει ὀπίσω μου ἔρχεσθαι, ἀπαρνησάσθω
ἑαυτὸν καὶ ἀράτω τὸν σταυρὸν αὐτοῦ καθ᾽ἡμέραν, καὶ
ἀκολουθείτω μοι. ὃς γὰρ ἂν θέλῃ τὴν ψυχὴν αὐτοῦ
σῶσαι, ἀπολέσει αὐτήν· ὃς δ᾽ἂν ἀπολέσῃ τὴν
ψυχὴν αὐτοῦ ἕνεκεν ἐμοῦ, οὗτος σώσει αὐτήν.

Looking at these passages, we see at once that Lk 9:23 is very close, as we might expect, to Mt 16:24ff. Lk 14:27, however, is not particularly close to Mt 10:38; indeed although the material is similar, it seems rather unlikely that they derive from the same proximate source. In other words the two Q passages may be from different sources, either literary or verbal.

To end the discussion of this section, let us now look back at the text of Mk 8:34ff:

Εἴ τις θέλει ὀπίσω μου ἐλθεῖν. ἀπαρνησάσθω ἑαυτὸν καὶ
ἀράτω τὸν σταυρὸν αὐτοῦ καὶ ἀκολουθείτω μοι. ὃς γὰρ ἐὰν θέλῃ τὴν
ψυχὴν αὐτοῦ σῶσαι ἀπολέσει αὐτήν. ὃς δ᾽ἂν ἀπολέσει τὴν ψυχὴν αὐτοῦ
ἕνεκεν [ἐμοῦ καὶ] τοῦ εὐαγγελίου σώσει αὐτήν.

This text preserves a pattern we might well expect. It is very close indeed to Lk 9, with the significant Markan addition of 'the Gospel' and the omission of the 'moralizing' καθ᾽ἡμέραν. It is equally close to Matthew. We should note, however, that where Mark and Luke speak of 'loving' and 'saving' one's life, Matthew in one place has 'loving' and 'finding'. But various (conflicting) explanations of this are possible. Matthew's text may be more 'unbalanced', but who can tell whether this is more or less primitive?

It seems that there were probably at least three versions of this story current: one which is reported by the Triple Tradition, one by Mt 10 and one by Lk 14. Can these three be collapsed into two? The most plausible way to do this, if we look at the Greek, would seem to be to regard *both* Matthew's versions as from the same source; both at least have the characteristic 'finding' of one's life. But this would entail, if Matthew used Mark, that he copied *the same passage*, once in Markan and once in non-Markan context, which is odd. But, it may be objected, if it is argued that Mt10:38 and Lk 14:27 were both from the document Q, the problem would disappear. However, the likelihood of this diminishes almost to vanishing point when we realize that, although Mt 10:37 parallels Lk 14:26, Mt 10:35 - 6 does not parallel Lk 14:24 - 5 (rather it parallels Lk 12:53). So if we invoke Q, we have to say that we have no idea of the order (or content) of much of Q at this point. And if Luke follows Matthew, his variant order deserves (but cannot achieve) an explanation. In any case our suspicions that Mt 10:37 - 8 is not closely (literarily?) parallel to Lk 14:26 - 7 will be confirmed by looking at Mt 10:37 and Lk 14:26. Mt 10:37 reads as follows: 'He who loves father and mother more than me is not worthy of me; and he who loves son or daughter more than me is not worthy of me'. Lk 14:26 reads more strangely at first sight: 'If anyone comes to me and does not hate his own father and mother and wife and children and brothers and sisters, yes and even his own life, he cannot be my disciple'.

Which of these versions is the more original, the more primitive? It might be claimed that the palm must go to Luke because his version is starker. Matthew, it would seem, has watered it down. On the other hand we would argue that Matthew's more 'ritual-sounding' approach, combined with an apparently more humane message, is more appropriate to Jesus. Or the two sayings could be words of Jesus uttered at different times. In favour of this latter interpretation is the fact that Luke refers to brothers, sisters, wife and self, where Matthew does not. The emphasis in Luke's version is on hating one's own life (= oneself). If Luke got his version from Matthew, or Matthew's source, where did he find the emphasis? And if Luke's version is the more accurate rendering of Q, or whatever, why did Matthew leave the self out? A more likely explanation is that the version of the story read by Matthew did not have this emphasis (or even mention) of the self.

Matthew, as we have seen, preserves the words about taking up one's cross twice. That is, of course, a not uncommon phenomenon, and the usual explanation is that he finds the material in two sources (e.g. Mark and Q) and thus simply reproduces it twice, forgetting (or disregarding) his earlier entry when he produces it a second time. But the explanation that the passages really did occur several times and were thus recorded several times is equally, or indeed rather more, likely. So that it may be the case not that two sources are involved, but two separate occasions. But, runs the reply, at least Mark is a source, for it is undeniable that Mt 16:24, Mk 8:34 and Lk 9:23 are all in the same context, that is, they occur just after the Confession at Caesarea Philippi and the first prediction of the Passion. However, it should be noticed that such a position for them is entirely natural. After Jesus has outlined his own future, he tells the disciples about carrying their cross. As I have already noted, Gaboury has identified this part of the Synoptics as Section C, where the sequence shows less variation. It looks, in fact, as though the tradition about the sequence of events in the Gospel was much more firmly fixed for this material before our Gospels reached their present form. In view of this and in view of the peculiarly appropriate place for our present texts, the sequence Mt 16:24 = Mk 8:34 etc. should not surprise us. Such similarity at this point looks plausible regardless of conditions of literary dependence whether of Mark on Matthew or Matthew on Mark. This is particularly plausible if we agree to eliminate the problem of three-way literary agreement by accepting at least Mark as among the sources of Luke.

(e) Matthew 11

There is no need to devote much space to this section. It is worthy of notice, however, that even though Matthew puts an end to Jesus' instructions to his disciples at 11:1, he does not return to the Markan sequence. Instead, throughout chapter 11 he occupies himself with material of a Q type, that is, material which occurs in variant forms in Luke but not in Mark. It has always been a puzzle for those who say that Mark derives from Matthew why Mark makes no use of this material. Why, in fact, does he neglect many passages which Luke uses if they were available to him? Certainly he did not have to use them, but his rationale is not always easy to comprehend. And the omission, if such it be, is hardly more striking elsewhere than in the case of John's question about the nature of Jesus and Jesus' words about John in the early part of Matthew 11 (2 - 19) (and in Luke 7). It was not only Palestinians, the presumed audience of Matthew, who would have been interested in the question of the relation of Jesus to John. Luke's audience is assumed to have a similar concern. And it is surprising indeed that Mark omits this material if he had a written version of it available to him, since he himself opens his whole Gospel with an account of John. Surprising, but acceptable, it may be argued. That is a matter of opinion; but at least there is some justification for claiming that the passage weighs against Mark knowing Matthew.

The same message about the relation of Mark and Matthew seems evident also from Mark's omission of the Lord's Prayer. This is perhaps the most striking omission of all, if Mark knew Matthew: a prayer specially ordained by Jesus himself. Mark's source could hardly have contained such material. Matthew and Luke present it, in rather different versions, in different parts of their narrative. Matthew puts it into the Sermon on the Mount (6:9 - 13), Luke into his 'Travel narrative' (11:1 - 4). There is therefore no means of identifying the original occasion or occasions of the prayer. Luke says that it was in response to a question about how to pray raised by one of the disciples.

Butler (following Rawlinson) claimed that, if not the Lord's Prayer, at least Mt 6:14, the explanatory next verse, is paralleled by Mk 11:25.[94] This passage of Mark provides the only occasion in Mark where God is called πατήρ ὁ ἐν τοῖς οὐρανοῖς (peculiar to Matthew except here). Now it is true that Mark also provides a parallel in this section for Matthew's ἀφιέναι παραπτώματα. But if Matthew is indeed the source of Mark here, Mark's behaviour in omitting the Our Father becomes more, not less, paradoxical and bizarre. A far more likely explanation is that Mt 6:14 and Mk 11:25 derive from some kind of common source. And an unwritten common source would the more readily account for the absence from Mark of the Lord's Prayer.[95]

8.   Matthew 13:24 - 52

Matthew 13:24 - 52 contains seven parables and various explanations. Most of this material is absent from Luke, though Luke does present the parables of the Mustard Seed and the Leaven elsewhere, and together (13:18 - 21). Three of the parables occur in Mark. Mark, however (and also Luke) completes chapter 4 and constructs the whole of chapter 5 with three sections (Stilling the Storm, The Gerasene Demoniac, Jairus' Daughter)[96] which appear elsewhere in Matthew. So in general we can say that, apart from the Mustard Seed and the Leaven we cannot even think of proving that Matthew is following a source Q also represented by Luke, and that we cannot therefore say that he is blending Mark with Q. At the very most we must consider the possibility that he is blending Mark with Q (unknown contents) and M (unknown contents). Now Streeter thought that the Leaven is Q material (i.e. that it is present in Luke and Matthew but absent from Mark). And he also thought that the Mustard Seed must be Q material too, since it contains a number of significant agreements of Matthew and Luke against Mark.[97] Which means that in the parable of the Mustard Seed Mark and Q overlap. Matthew combines Mark with Q, says the Two-Documentarian. But if Matthew is using Q here, in this part of chapter 13, he is not only using Q, since many of the parallels occur neither in Luke nor in Mark. So if Matthew has a source M for much of what was supposed to be Q, it is equally likely that that source covers the so-called Q (and Markan?) sections as well. So that although Matthew may be condensing Mark and Q, it is equally likely that his source is quite independent, as it was in his two earlier chapters. It is in fact more likely (though not very likely) that Mark depends on Matthew than vice versa.

When we began this chapter, our intention was to carry further some of the ideas of Chapter Two. In investigating Mk 2:23 - 6:13, or at least large parts of it, and in comparing it with similar material in Matthew we have noted the following:

(i) Gaboury is right in believing that it is hard to see that Matthew is following Mark's basic sequence. Other possibilities may be invoked as more plausible explanations of Matthew's order.

(ii) Even in passages where Matthew's order is parallel to Mark's there are good reasons for denying that Matthew is following Mark, even where there is close verbal similarity.

(iii) There may be indications in this section that Jesus repeated himself, and that such repetitions were recorded in the tradition. It is therefore methodologically incorrect to assume *a priori* that similarity, or even identity of wording, entails literary derivation. In Synoptic criticism, where we are dealing with both verbal and written traditions, the canons of purely literary *Quellenforschung* can be applied misleadingly.

(iv) There is good ground to suspect that in most of the material covered by chapters 2 to 5 of Mark, whether the other Synoptics follow 'Markan' sequence or not, Matthew does not follow Mark.

(v) There is little indication in these sections that the contrary literary thesis holds, namely that Mark follows Matthew.

4

MORE SKIMPINGS AND BOWDLERIZINGS IN MATTHEW

This chapter is primarily concerned with the claim that there are a number of passages where a comparison between Mark and Matthew shows that Matthew deliberately 'softened' or 'watered-down' a text of Mark which for one reason or another he found unacceptable. In order to give opponents the benefit of the doubt where possible, I shall say nothing of the fact that those who advance this claim nowadays tend to forget the possibility that Matthew is 'watering down' not Mark but Mark's source. I shall, however, also touch on the broader question of those passages where Matthew's version may seem not bowdlerized, but rather an inadequate summary of a graphic and detailed Markan original. I shall attempt to show in a number of well-known instances that claims about Matthew's dependence on Mark that have been based on such 'observation' are exaggerated and misleading, indeed that normally no conclusions about chronological priority can be based on the evidence available. In particular I shall reject the assumption that a 'softer' passage is necessarily a 'softened' passage, and *a fortiori* that it is a later passage.

We have already come across some of these problems in our earlier analyses; in particular we have noted that in some parts of the Synoptics it looks as though Mark might be a summary based on Matthew, and elsewhere the converse might be the case. In fact we have argued that literary dependence cannot be assumed in such passages. The purpose of this chapter is to pursue this same line of enquiry, focusing our attention on a number of traditionally difficult texts. Finally we note that not only do Markan priorists tend to assume that a skimpy version must be an epitome of a more detailed one, they also rarely allow for the possibility that stories may be embellished, with or without justification, in later versions;[98] or that we may be dealing not with an epitome but with an alternative version. Some of the examples that I shall select in Matthew are in Markan context, others are outside it.

1. Stilling the Storm (Mt 8:23 - 7, Mk 4:35 - 41, Lk 8:22 - 5)

Sometimes alleged waterings-down of Mark by Matthew have been virtually fabricated. The Stilling of the Storm is an example of this procedure, a procedure designed, we recall, to show that Matthew found Mark's more graphic version too strong meat. In this case Matthew diverges from the order of Mark and Luke, though clearly the same story is involved and all three Evangelists put the accounts into Gaboury's section D. Mark's version is rather more graphic: he provides details such as that Jesus was asleep on a cushion, which look like eyewitness material, and, some say, he includes a rebuke to Jesus by the disciples which Luke and Matthew have toned down. Now it is certain that verbally the stories in all three Synoptics are very close, but there are also interesting divergences of vocabulary. Consider the following:

Mt	Mk	Lk
σεισμὸς μέγας	λαῖλαψ ἀνέμου μεγάλη	κατέβη (different verb)
		λαῖλαψ ἀνέμου
τὸ πλοῖον καλύπτεσθαι	γεμίζεσθαι τὸ πλοῖον	συνεπληροῦντο
ὀλιγόπιστοι	οὔπω ἔχετε πίστιν	ποῦ ἡ πίστις ὑμῶν
	(in different place)	

The variations are slight. Certainly they could be caused by variants from a single original written source; and there is no denying that Mark's is the most graphic version. But 'most graphic' does not equal 'necessarily earlier', and in view of the perhaps insignificant variations we have observed, it is not easy to see why another variant should not be equally trivial and uninformative. That variant is that whereas Mark has the disciples say 'Don't you care that we perish', Matthew has 'Lord, save us, we perish'. From such tiny misconceptions major errors are born, for far from being different in tone, both these remarks could have been made quite appropriately in sequence: 'Lord, save us, we perish; don't you care that we perish'. There is no profit for Markan priorists (or any other priorists here).

2. The Rich Young Man and the Question about the Good (Mt 19:16 - 30, Mk 10:17 - 31, Lk 18:18 - 30)

This section is much like the previous one in that largely unwarranted conclusions about it have frequently been drawn from quite inadequate evidence. It has, however, been discussed recently by Sanders,[99] whose conclusion that it affords no evidence about the possible priority of Mark or Matthew (beyond what *may* be deducible from Mt 19:30 (Mk 10:31)) I largely accept. Sanders, however, is at least impressed by the argument of Butler [100] that in Matthew this final verse is the introduction to the following parable, not the conclusion of the history of the rich young man, while Mark has mistakenly taken it as a conclusion, omitting the passage that follows. Butler thus sees this as an argument for the priority of Matthew to Mark, noting that Luke presents the *logion* elsewhere (13:30).

But the part of this section in which I am more interested is the initial question of the rich young man, and Jesus' response. In both Mark and Luke, the question is, 'Good Teacher, what shall I do . . .?' And the reply is 'Why do you call me good? No one is good but God alone'. Matthew, however, has 'Teacher, what good deed must I do . . .?', and 'Why do you ask me about what is good? One there is who is good'.[101] Matthew, it has been argued, out of respect, has suppressed the Markan version where Jesus appears to reject the title 'good'. But it might well be argued that the Markan version does no such thing. Rather Jesus is raising with the rich young man - whom, after all, he appears to have considered a possible disciple - the question of his being more than man. And we should recall that this text comes after the 'Confession' of Peter and Jesus' endorsement of that confession before the other disciples. On this interpretation Matthew may have misunderstood Mark, but he can hardly be said to have suppressed Mark's version out of reverence.

There is a further point: on the traditional interpretation Matthew's version is more coherent than Mark's if we consider the reference to the commandments which follows. In Matthew the question 'What shall I do?' is asked. Jesus, perhaps surprised, replies, 'Why ask me? Am I the source of goodness [perhaps raising the same question about divinity as Mark]? God is good; he has already given you the commandments.' In Mark's version the question 'Why do you call me good?' is almost irrelevant on any interpretation except the one we have sketched. If Mark is to be taken in a 'less reverential fashion', Jesus' question implies merely that he is correcting the young man. And that would only be plausible if the author of Mark wanted to give the impression that Jesus did not claim divinity - which is patently not his intention. In brief then we would argue that in both the Matthaean and the Markan versions Jesus raises the question of his divinity. The tradition about how this was done varies slightly, but the 'tone' of the passages is similar. And in view of Sanders' findings about the rest of this section (which is well into Gaboury's section C) we must insist that there is nothing here to upset the verdict that there are no grounds for assigning priority at this point. This verdict is particularly significant in view of the fact that the story of the rich young man is one of the 'basic Gospel' texts identified in Chapter One.

3.   Jairus' Daughter (Mt 9:18 - 26, Mk 5:21 - 43, Lk 8:40 - 56)

Mark and Luke place this story after the 'Gerasene' demoniac and shortly before the end of the section D. Matthew puts it in a much earlier place, after the Question about Fasting and the New Wine in Old Wineskins. There seems no particular reason for Matthew's position. He either put Jairus where he did because, rightly or wrongly, he thought that this was the correct chronological sequence, or because some tradition had it there; it is hard to see why he should have put it where he has on grounds of appropriateness of context. The context he uses is not, admittedly, inappropriate, but neither is it particularly appropriate. In other words if Matthew were following Mark, it is hard to see why he has changed Mark's order in this case; and if Mark were supposed to be following Matthew, the same point could be made.

As for the story itself, the setting of all the Synoptics is probably the same, that is, Capernaum, but the details in Mark and Luke are much more impressive than in Matthew. Matthew's version is certainly abbreviated, if not inaccurate. Both Mark and Luke mention Jairus by name; Matthew does not. Mark and Luke say that he was one of the rulers of the synagogue (ἀρχισυνάγωγος, ἄρχων τῆς συναγωγῆς); Matthew merely describes him as a ruler (ἄρχων), thus omitting a particularly significant fact. More strikingly still Mark and Luke indicate that Jairus urged Jesus to come to his house because his daughter was dying; Matthew says that Jairus said that his daughter had just died. To be consistent with this last point Matthew naturally omits the later material in Mark and Luke whereby while Jairus is speaking to Jesus, a messenger comes up and informs them that the girl is now dead. Thus, it might be argued, Matthew increases the amount of reverence for Jesus' powers in that in his version Jairus recognizes Jesus' ability to raise the girl from the dead. Minor details, perhaps comparatively unimportant, are also absent in Matthew. He declines to tell us, for example, that Jesus took only Peter, James and John with him; and he declines to mention the actual words (even in the Greek translation offered by Luke) with which Jesus raised the girl. Finally, he omits the interesting and significant detail that Jesus told the girl's parents to give her something to eat.

In all three Synoptics, the account of Jairus' daughter encapsulates the healing of a woman with a haemorrhage. Again Matthew's version is extraordinarily brief; in particular he omits all reference to Jesus noticing that 'the power' had gone out of him. Luke, it is interesting to note here, has added in the name of Peter, suppressed by Mark - an indication, perhaps, that he had another source with which he touched up Mark when he found it necessary. But if he had, that source was not Matthew, for Matthew has no mention of Peter either. And it is possible, of course, that Peter's name is a mere later gloss in the transmitted text of Luke, though in this case the context makes that unlikely.

What are the effects of Matthew's 'omissions', and what can we deduce
from placing Mark and Matthew side by side? One conclusion is fairly clear:
it is rather unlikely that Mark's text is a developed version of Matthew's.
If it is, why does he change Jairus' original report? If Matthew said the
girl was dead, why does Mark have her dying? Perhaps, it might be said,
Mark is deliberately *correcting* Matthew. That is possible, but if so, then
he also has *other* material which he can add when he later describes the
actual report of her death. And if he follows this material at the later stage
because it is more reliable, it is most likely that he would have followed it
all through. The additional material, let us note, contains both words of
Jesus and narrative. In fact if anyone holds that Mark *used* Matthew in
this complete section, both in the story of Jairus' daughter and in that of
the woman with a haemorrhage, he has to say that Mark prefers Matthew
for the scraps which Matthew has and then always fills him out or follows
another source *only* where there is no Matthew - a most unlikely description of Mark's procedure in the undoubtedly graphic story which he nar-
rates.

What then of the more likely theory in this case, namely that Matthew
used Mark? Obviously it is possible, and if true it would, as has often been
observed, militate against Matthew's Gospel being the work of Matthew.
That, however, is not our concern. But let us take note of what a clumsy
abridgement he has made, if that is what it is. If Matthew had Mark available, why has he left out the reference to the synagogue? Why has he deliberately changed the story so that Jairus tells Jesus his daughter is dead
(the miracle, in any case, involves the death of the girl, so there is no question of Matthew merely expanding on the miraculous element)? If
Matthew is précising Mark, we have to assume an extreme carelessness -
the problem has appeared before - and to ask ourselves whether such carelessness is likely. But it may be argued that Matthew is only going on what
he remembers of Mark. But if we fall back on that, we may as well say
that Matthew is remembering the story of Jairus. There is then no reason
why it should be Mark's story of Jairus that we are concerned with.

Here we have a supposed précis of Mark. But the conclusions drawn
from it by Markan priorists are no more impressive than those drawn from
the passage we discussed in an earlier chapter about the purpose of parables,[102] where we found that Matthew's alleged softening of the text was
more plausibly explained as due to different translations of an Aramaic
particle.

4. The rejection of Jesus at Nazareth (Mt 13:53 - 8, Mk 6:1 - 6a, Lk 4:16 - 30)

Matthew and Mark agree in placing this section near the end of Gaboury's section D, though Matthew, whose 'section D' closes with the Rejection, puts it after the Parable of the Householder and Mark after Jairus' Daughter. Luke, on the other hand, produces a rather different version immediately after Jesus has begun to preach in Galilee.[103] There is a great deal of material in Luke which is to be found neither in Mark nor in Matthew, and which thus provides good evidence that another source was available, even if Luke did after all use Mark and/or Matthew as well. But what of Mark and Matthew? Verbally and contextually the texts are very close, though there are curious variants. Jesus is the son of a carpenter in Matthew, and a carpenter in Mark.[104] The most significant of these variants, it is said, is that whereas Mark says that Jesus was *unable* to perform a mighty work that day, Matthew prefers to say that he did not do many mighty works. It is then alleged[105] that Matthew has watered-down Mark. But this is not a straightforward or self-evident statement of the position. There may be no difference in the two accounts. Both say that Jesus' failure to do great works was 'because of their unbelief'. And Mark does not say that he could do *no* mighty work, but that he could do no mighty work except that he laid hands on a few sick people and healed them. So the net effect is very little different from what we have in Matthew. Of course, one might agree that the clause 'except that he laid hands on a few . . .' is an interpolation or developed version of the original 'pure' Markan text, but at this point we have to ask how much guesswork is acceptable merely in the interest of saving a theory, in this case the theory that Matthew watered-down something he found unacceptable in Mark. For that theory could only look credible if there was regular evidence of Matthew engaging in such waterings-down. And there is not. What there is, of course, is the fact that Mark has less miraculous events in his narrative than Matthew, and therefore, it is argued, he must be more primitive. Once the question-begging nature of this reasoning is recognized, we shall avoid the temptation to read Matthew as deliberately watering-down supposed 'weaknesses' in Jesus as presented in the Gospel of Mark. For in this passage at least, it is hard to see that such weaknesses exist in the Markan original as compared with what Matthew himself presents. So all we are left with in the case of this passage is that this is one of those texts where Mark and Matthew have close verbal similarities and place the events in a rather similar context. No conclusions can safely be drawn from that as to their relationship.

5. Healing an epileptic boy (Mt 17:14 - 20, Mk 9:14 - 29, Lk 9:37 - 43a)
This story, though in Gaboury's section C, has a number of parallels with the account of Jairus' Daughter and is worth comparing with it. In this case, however, we notice that Luke's version is almost as abbreviated as Matthew's - an indication that he does not primarily follow Mark in his

account - and also exhibits a number of additions and subtractions. It is possible that the origin of the story in Matthew and Luke is to be identified, while Luke seems to prefer another source to Mark (assuming that he has Mark available). But although the *origin* of the story in Luke and Matthew may be identical, it is hard to show that Luke has used *Matthew* as his source. Or if he has, he has blended that source with other materials and omitted some striking details of Matthew's account, such as that the boy often fell in a fit into the fire (Mt 17:14). Again when we compare Mark and Matthew the same dilemma confronts us as confronted us in dealing with Jairus' Daughter. Mark, if he expanded Matthew, had a lot of other evidence, so much indeed that it is hard to see why he should use Matthew's inferior account at all. More likely he did not do so. There remains the other alternative, namely that Matthew epitomized Mark. If he did, let us see the results: (1) Matthew has recast Mark's order; (2) the striking words of the father and Jesus' reply about unbelief are omitted; (3) Mt 17:20 is added; (4) an especially enfeebled version is produced. Again with respect to (4) we may note that such an enfeebled version would be better explained if Matthew had a source much inferior to Mark as his base. If he uses Mark, he has done a very poor job. The problem with verse 20 is more complicated. A rather similar saying of Jesus, this time approximately paralleled in Mark, occurs at Mt 21:21. So if Matthew read Mark, he found this saying at the equivalent of 21:21 (i.e. Mk11:23), not at the equivalent of 17:20. Yet he has it at 17:20, though Mark does not, and Luke has his parallel elsewhere (17:6). But if Matthew derives 17:20 from a non-Markan source (and probably not the source of Luke), it is highly likely that the whole section comes from somewhere other than Mark. True, verse 20 could be an interpolation, but it runs very naturally after verse 19, and there is no reason (other than a desire to beg the question) for supposing that it is incorrectly placed.

We have now considered a number of sections where it has been commonly believed that Matthew has produced an expurgated version of Mark. We have found no reason to believe in such expurgations and we have noticed rather that these sections seem to fall into a pattern very similar to that which we have already observed in earlier chapters. Often no conclusions can safely be drawn about literary dependence. Sometimes the theory that Matthew depends on Mark entails extraordinary carelessness on the part of Matthew. Sometimes the theory that Mark depends on Matthew entails an extraordinarily unlikely genesis for the brilliant and graphic Markan narrative. Sometimes it appears that the source for Matthew is not available to (or is unused by) the other Evangelists.

5

A TURNING POINT IN THE TRADITION
(Mt 14:1, Mk 6:14, Lk 9:7)

Gaboury has argued that Mt 14:1 (and parallels) marks the end of the section where the sequence of events in the three Synoptics is rather disorderly, and where a traditional order had not been firmly fixed at the time of the composition of our canonical texts. If that thesis is correct, and a new stability begins at this point, we might expect to find some evidence of the transition, and it would certainly seem likely *a priori* that an investigation of the opening stories of the 'set' narrative sequence would be fruitful. The texts run as follows:

Herod thinks that Jesus			
is John risen:	Mt 14:1 - 2;	Mk 6:14 - 16;	Lk 9:7 - 9
Death of John the Baptist	Mt 14:3 - 12;	Mk 6:17 - 29;	(Lk 3:19 - 20)
Return of Twelve		Mk 6:30;	Lk 9:10a
Feeding the 5000	Mt 14:13 - 21;	Mk 6:31 - 44;	Lk 9:10a - 17
Walking on the Water,			
Gennesaret, on			
Defilement:	Mt 14:22 - 15:20;	Mk 6:45 - 7:23	
The Syrophoenician Woman:	Mt 15:21 - 8;	Mk 7:24 - 30	

1. Herod, John and the Return

Both Mark and Matthew place Herod's mistake about Jesus shortly after the rejection of Jesus at Nazareth, though Mark interposes a passage about the sending out of the Twelve which, as we have seen earlier, Matthew inserts at 10:1ff. In the narrative of Herod's mistake, Matthew's version is the most abbreviated, though he gets Herod's title (tetrarch) correct[106] a detail unnoticed by Mark, who has the vaguer 'king' (βασιλεύς), but recorded by Luke. Attention has focused, however, on the 'flashback' sequence of John's execution that follows, for this scene, omitted by Luke presumably because of his earlier reference to John's arrest, is presented in the same manner in Mark and Matthew. It is generally agreed, once again, that Mark's version of the incident is superior; the account of Herod's wish to save John's life but his unwillingness to go back on his oath is

consistent in Mark, whereas Matthew attempts to combine this with a
statement that Herod himself (rather than Herodias, as in Mark) wanted
to put John to death (14:5). But even more curious is that at the end of
the narrative of John's death, Matthew seems to forget that he is giving us
a flashback. In Mark the account of John's death is completed and the
narrative then goes back to the Twelve, to their return to Jesus with a report on their preaching mission. Luke's presentation also refers to the report of the Twelve, but of course Matthew has to proceed differently, because he has placed the sending out of the Twelve in a quite different
place in his narrative.

There is no doubt that Matthew's version of these transactions is in confusion, and it is most unlikely that his confused account is the basis of
Mark's clear-cut narrative. On the other hand we have a recurrence of our
old problem, in a particularly acute form: if Matthew was working from
Mark, his own textual chaos is incomprehensible. If, on the other hand,
he is either vaguely remembering events himself, or relying on unwritten
(or garbled written) tradition, the confusion is far more readily explicable.
It might be argued that since Matthew had altered the position of the
sending out of the Twelve, he was faced with the necessity of doing what
he could with the remainder of Mark's narrative in this section, and that
he simply botched the not-too difficult job which confronted him. But
Matthew's activities would have been far more intelligible (were he using
a written source like Mark) if he had put the sending of the Twelve in
Mark's place, thus avoiding all the difficulties. Since Matthew seems to
have had no particularly strong reason for shifting Mark's account of the
sending of the Twelve which might be used to justify his procedures, the
reasonable conclusion must be that he did not use Mark as his source in
either passage. Rather he had quite other reasons, independent of Mark
but substantial, for selecting the order of events he has given us. We are
still, of course, left with the confusion in Matthew's text, which needs
explanation. But explanation seems hardly possible on the assumption
that Mark is his source.

2. The Feeding of the 5000

All three Synoptics present the story of the Feeding of the 5000, and Mark
and Luke tie it to the return of the Twelve. I observed in Chapter One
that this is a possible candidate for membership in a 'basic Gospel' and that
it is possible that it earned its peculiar place in the narrative because it was
treated as a 'Eucharistic' prefiguration of the Passion narrative. But although the story occurs in all three Synoptics, there are few close verbal
agreements in the early part. We have already argued that the sources uti-
lized by Mark and Matthew for the return of the Twelve are distinct; we

can now see that in what follows, although the same event (the Feeding) is being described, the accounts are very different. This constitutes striking evidence in favour of Gaboury, for it may be argued not that the sequence is set by tradition, but that an Evangelist may still feel free to resort to different versions of the tradition. We may notice, for example, that whereas neither Matthew nor Mark identify the locale of the miracle, Luke places it at Bethsaida (9:10) - though Mark does mention Bethsaida soon after his account (missing in Luke) of the Feeding of the 4000 (8:22). In general we notice that there are very few verbal agreements in the early part of this narrative between Mark and Luke or between Luke and Matthew. In the later part of the story, however, i.e. in the 'consecration narrative', verbal parallels become impressive, probably reflecting usage in the Christian communities. Our overall impression of the passage, though, is that we have a section which has a mandatory position in the Gospel sequence, but where there are three distinct traditions at work for the details. It may be legitimate to refer to this passage as in the Triple Tradition, but that should not be taken to imply literary relationships between the three versions. Matthew does not depend on Mark, nor Mark on Matthew, and Luke, who operates with blocks of source-material, is dependent on neither of them.

3.   The 'Syrophoenician' Woman (Mt 15:21 - 8, Mk 7:24 - 30)

After the Feeding of the 5000, Luke moves directly to the beginning of the most important stage in Jesus' career, inaugurated by the 'confession' of Peter that he is the Christ. Matthew and Mark have other material, in the same sequence, but often different in detail. One of the more interesting sections of this material from our present point of view is the story of the 'Syrophoenician' woman. The account occurs in the same sequence in these two Synoptics, but it is most unlikely that either one is the source of the other. Clearly there is a common tradition, which Luke has suppressed, of Jesus going to the districts of Tyre and Sidon.[107] There he is approached by a non-Jewish woman whose daughter is possessed. At first he is unwilling to heal the girl, but later, because of her mother's faith, he does so.[108] The story in both versions indicates a tradition that in the early stages of his mission Jesus wished to call only Jews (a theme we have already found in an earlier part of Matthew missing in Mark), but that he later began to widen it. A glance at the Synopticon, however, indicates that within this general common theme, only a few of the words spoken between Jesus and the woman are identical in the two accounts. In other words there was a strong tradition about the kind of language used, and the tradition has come down to us in both the Markan and the Matthaean versions, but beyond that there is very little agreement in detail. It is frequently pointed out that, for whatever reason, Matthew, in speaking of the woman as Canaanite, locates the events in an Old Testament 'context', while Mark reflects the contemporary political scene. And indeed there are a number of interesting details given by Matthew, such as the impatience of the disciples with the woman; though on the other hand the ending of the story is banal in Matthew, but fitted out with circumstantial detail in Mark: 'She went home and found the child lying in bed, and the demon gone . . .'. On previous occasions we have found now Matthew, now Mark (often Matthew) looking like an epitome; here we find that in different parts of the story each author looks as though he is presenting an abbreviated account. And we should notice too the particularly significant fact that even Jesus' words are different in one important respect. Matthew says that he said to the woman, 'Your faith is great'. The idea is implicit in Mark, explicit in Matthew. What must we conclude? That Matthew has adapted Mark? That would be more convincing if throughout the passage it appeared plausible, as Bultmann supposed, that Matthew has debased a Markan original. And it cannot be denied that this is just possible. Far more likely, however, is the alternative that both Matthew and Mark are heirs of a common tradition. Of course this in no way commits us on the question of how long a tradition we have, or how near either Mark or Matthew is to the 'originals' of the stories they recount, or even whether the traditions are oral or written.

We have been inspecting a group of passages between Mt 14:1 (Mk 6:14) and Mt 16:13 (Mk 8:27), from Herod's mistake to the confession at Caesarea Philippi. A number of interesting features have emerged, which we should now attempt to summarize:

(i) Luke's narrative is of very limited scope when compared with Mark or Matthew. He tells us about Herod's mistake, omits the death of John (which he has mentioned elsewhere), alludes to the return of the disciples and describes the feeding of the five thousand, which he seems to locate, wrongly, at Bethsaida. He then proceeds directly to the 'confession', for which no location is given, thereby omitting, among other things, Jesus' entire journey to Tyre and Sidon. It can certainly be said that the basic sequence of all this is Markan, but it is as certain as anything can be in Synoptic criticism that Luke does not follow Mark. Nor is there much reason to suppose he follows Matthew either, for although he knows Matthew's correct information about Herod's title of tetrarch, and in general it is conceivable that his section 9:7 - 9 is an amalgam of Matthew and Mark, this possibility is made far more unlikely by his obvious

desertion of Mark and/or Matthew in his account of the
five thousand. And it is certainly remarkable that an author
following either Matthew or Mark for the confession should
even omit to tell us where it occurred. It is in fact reasonably
certain that Luke is manipulating a tradition in this section
which insists on mention of Herod, but then proceeds directly
to the confession and its 'necessary' precursor, the Feeding of
the 5000.

(ii) Reflection on Luke shows us that within a basic sequence
there existed traditional versions of this part of Jesus' career
other than what is recorded by Mark and Matthew. Reflection
on Mark and Matthew, particularly in the passages we have
considered in detail, indicates that they are dependent on
largely parallel but distinct source traditions. To observe this
parallelism again we may look at the route followed by Jesus
in Mt 14:13 - 16:13 and compare it with that of Mk 6:30 - 8:27.

Mt	Mk
Lonely place (5000)	Lonely place (5000)
To the other side	To Bethsaida
Over to Gennesaret	Over to Gennesaret
To Tyre and Sidon (Canaanite woman)	To Tyre and Sidon (Syrophoenician woman)
Along sea of Galilee (4000)	To sea of Galilee through Decapolis (4000)
To Magadan (probably Magdala)	To Dalmanutha (probably corrupt)[109]
To other side	To other side, on to Bethsaida (miracle of blind man)

(iii) The most important point which must be made about this
section of the Synoptics is that the more one emphasizes the
basically common sequence, the more striking are the verbal
variations within that common sequence, and the stronger the
evidence these provide against a solution of the Synoptic
problem in terms of a purely literary model. Even in the
earlier sections of text (Gaboury's section D) we have found it
necessary to pay attention to such divergences and to argue that
their implications have not been taken sufficiently seriously. In
Gaboury's section C, and increasingly so as we get into long
stretches where all three Synoptics give versions of the same story
in the same place, such implications become more serious than ever.

6

SOME PASSAGES ABOUT PETER IN MATTHEW

We have already found some indication in the fourteenth and fifteenth chapters of Matthew that in these crucial sections of the narrative Matthew and Mark rely on different traditions. I now propose to inspect five passages in chapters 14 to 18 of Matthew dealing with Peter which may seem to point in the same direction. Matthew, in telling the same stories as Mark, is able to use material about Peter which, for some reason, is absent from the parallel passages of Mark. Since all these passages are in close proximity to one another, it might seem that an explanation is required. This is particularly true if we accept the ancient view, as I do, that Mark's Gospel is to be connected with Peter's preaching. I shall argue further that the fact that there are five such passages makes them of particular significance; had there been only one or two it would have been easier to claim that the appearance of Peter's name is due merely to the desire of redactors to give heightened verisimilitude to the narrative by adding in personal touches.

Let us now look at the passages in detail:

1. Mt 14:28 - 31
These lines form part of the story of Jesus walking on the water. Much of the narrative of the story is very close in Matthew and Mark, but it does not occur in Luke; Mark, however, has no reference to Peter at all. Matthew, on the other hand, tells how Peter invited Jesus to call him to walk on the water, but that after trying to do so, he began to sink. Peter called out to Jesus to save him, and Jesus, catching him by the hand, comments, 'Man of little faith, why did you doubt?' Of this account we may notice the following:

  (a) It is a story where Peter's impetuosity and weakness of faith is shown;

  (b) it is a characteristically 'Matthaean' addition in the eyes of those who see Matthew's Gospel more 'disfigured' by the miraculous when compared with Mark's;

(c) we are dealing not merely with the addition of the
name Peter, but with an incident.[110]

2. Mt 15:15

This time we have merely the name 'Peter' in Matthew, where Mark refers
to the disciples. It is interesting to observe, however, that Matthew's text
throughout this section is rather more abbreviated than Mark's. Yet it is
Matthew who has the specific name. Although more vague in general, it is
more specific in this particular.

3. Mt 16:17 - 19, etc.

This is, of course, the most famous of all the 'Petrine' additions.[111] The
'confession' story, as we have already observed, occurs in all three
Synoptics. Matthew and Mark place it at Caesarea Philippi; Luke gives no
indication of locale. Peter, in all three accounts, identifies Jesus as the
Christ, but Jesus' reply, including the words, 'You are Peter and on this
rock I will build my church . . . I will give you the keys of the kingdom',
etc., occurs only in Matthew. Naturally there are those who argue that
this is a 'later' interpolation in the original, in part because of the occur-
rence of the word 'Church' (ἐκκλησία)[112]   But there is no reason yet
available why Jesus should not have used this Septuagintal term,[113] or
envisaged an organization of believers. In any case it is strange to find a
'non-Markan' insertion advocating the importance of Peter in a Markan
narrative - if, that is, Palestinian Matthew is based on Mark. In fact for a
variety of reasons, not least because Luke does not copy the Matthaean
tradition, it is clear that Matthew got this material from a source peculiar
to himself. And there is no reason why this source should not be the
source of the whole account of the 'confession' at Caesarea Philippi. But
why should not Matthew merely have added Q to Mark? Presumably it
cannot be identified as Q, since there is no trace of it in Luke.

Now if Mt 16:17 - 19 are from a source unique to Matthew, what about
20 - 3? Verse 20 is perhaps merely a paraphrase in Matthew, perhaps dependent on the same source as Mark, but not necessarily so. Verse 21
refers to Jerusalem where the other Synoptics do not. In 22 - 3 Matthew
retains some more of Peter's actual words which are not present in Mark:
'God forbid, Lord! This shall never happen to you'.[114] And Jesus' reply
is slightly different too. If anything Mark looks like an epitome of Matthew
here playing down, among other things, the role of Peter; but it is probably not an epitome. The most likely explanation is that for the whole
narrative of the 'confession', Matthew is dependent on (or identifiable
with) M, a source supplying a good deal of 'Petrine material' absent from
Mark.

4. Mt 17:24 - 7

Here is another story, this time about the temple-tax, which occurs in
Matthew alone. It contains an implicit miraculous element, for Jesus in-
vites Peter to cast a hook into the sea; he will then catch a fish with a
shekel in its mouth for the payment of the temple-tax. Butler, grotesquely,
claims that Mark knows this section because Matthew tells us that it occurred at Capernaum and gives a reference to 'home', while Mark has references to Capernaum and 'in the house' at 9:33, the next section, which is
a Triple Tradition passage. On such slender threads are theories hung;
there is no reason why such premises should demonstrate that Mark knew
Matthew.

5. Mt 18:21 - 2

This looks like a Q passage, occurring in this case in Matthew and Luke, but
not in Mark. But the two versions are different. Luke merely lists the
saying 'if he sins against you seven times in the day . . .' among other sayings of Jesus; Matthew mentions a question by Peter 'How often shall my
brother sin against me and I forgive him?'   And the words of Jesus differ
substantially too. It is quite possible that the 'source' of Matthew and
Luke is different; certainly the context is different. And there is no particular reason why Luke should have suppressed Peter's name if he had found
it in Matthew or in any other source. It is therefore possible to add this
passage to our others as coming from a 'source' close to, or concerned with,
Peter and unavailable to (or neglected by) the writers of the other
Synoptics.

Thus we have five passages, in fairly close proximity in Matthew, where
there is special attention to Peter. Of these five, one (the confession at
Caesarea Philippi) is in a section which occurs in some version in all three
Gospels, two (Mt 14:28 - 31 and 15:15, the latter a minimal passage) are
in sections common to Matthew and Mark but not in Luke, one is in what
has been labelled a Q passage, and the last is a passage peculiar to Matthew
alone. This divergence of types of material, combined with the close proximity of these sections in Matthew's narrative, points strongly to the position that Matthew is using a personal and unique source in chapters 14 to
18. What that source may be we need not consider at the present time,
but if we accept it, we cannot but be puzzled at the omission of these
Petrine passages from both Mark and Luke. And in view of the diverse
nature of the Petrine material, it is more difficult to argue that these sections of Matthew are merely glosses and additions to a Markan original.
For the question then arises as to why there are so many glosses on this
part of Mark of this particular kind. And in any case why should Matthew

gloss Mark with Petrine material? Perhaps it might be argued that he represents a 'Petrine' party in the Palestinian church of the middle or late
first century; but the difficulty of that is that apart from the Caesarea
Philippi section, the new references to Peter do not show him in any particularly creditable light. They could hardly be described as the documents
of a faction consciously or half-consciously promoting a monarchical epis-
copate. The most likely hypothesis is that this material goes back to a
continuous narrative independent of the written Gospels of Matthew and
Mark, though not, of course, necessarily co-extensive with the whole of
those works.[115] This conclusion further reinforces our earlier deductions,
based particularly on discussion of the Feeding of the 5000 and the
'Syrophoenician' woman, about the nature of the material in this crucial
section of the Synoptics where Gaboury has claimed to find an increasingly set sequence of Gospel events.

7

FROM CAESAREA PHILIPPI TO
THE BURIAL OF JESUS

It would obviously be possible to discuss every line and indeed every word
of the Synoptics in search of literary derivation, but after a while the exercise becomes monotonous. I have already noted that in the later sections
of the Synoptics it has been observed that variation in the order of pericopae between Matthew, Mark and Luke (apart, of course, from Luke's
'Travel Narrative') is very much reduced. For whatever reason, the general
order of material in many of these sections is more obviously fixed. It
might look, therefore, as if literary dependence is available as an explanation of this. I believe, however, that the hypothesis of such dependence
in the case of Mark and Matthew is not only unnecessary but that there
are many passages which cast doubt upon it, and I shall discuss a number
of them. In a sense nothing new will be added to our earlier evidence, but
it may be of interest to see that similar results are obtainable from one
end of the Synoptics to the other.

1. Divorce
Both Matthew (19:1 - 12) and Mark (10:1 - 12) have a section on divorce
after Jesus leaves Galilee for Judaea and eventually Jerusalem. Luke, who
shortly rejoins the Synoptic sequence after his 'Travel Narrative', omits
this section, probably because he has already given us teaching on divorce
a little earlier (at 16:18). The setting of the question about divorce ad-
dressed to Jesus by the Pharisees is similar in these two Gospels, though
the sequence of discussion is different. In Mark Jesus' counterquestion
'What did Moses command you?' precedes his remarks about God creating
male and female; in Matthew it follows them. But more notoriously, the
question put by the Pharisees differs in each account. Mark has 'Is it lawful for a man to divorce his wife?' (10:2), while Matthew read 'Is it lawful
[for a man] to divorce (ἀπολῦσαι) one's wife for any cause?' (19:3). It
is commonly supposed that in the replies Matthew allows 'unchastity' as a
ground of 'divorce' and then passes on to observe that if the 'divorce' is
followed by remarriage, then the man commits adultery. On this interpretation 'divorce' would mean separation, and the emphasis would be on

the ban on remarriage. Mark has nothing to say about unchastity, but
merely makes the point that 'divorce' followed by remarriage is adultery.
He then adds that if the wife 'divorces' her husband, the same rules apply.
Various comments are regularly made on these passages, but we need note
only the following: (1) If Mark copied Matthew, he has very oddly omitted
the phrase 'except for unchastity'. A possible explanation of this would be
to argue that 19:9 is a later version in Matthew, since the section on divorce
is already rounded off by a 'Semitic *inclusio*' at 19:8. On this view 19:9
would be a mere cross-reference (added later?) to Mt 5:32.[116] The difficulty about this is that there is no manuscript support for 19:9 not being
(in some form) part of the original text of Matthew. Assuming that Mt
19:9 is original Matthew, however, it might still possibly be argued that
Mark need not have included the unchastity clause if he was only interested in insisting that 'divorce plus remarriage equals adultery'. (2) If
Matthew copied Mark, then not only has he added the 'except for unchastity', but he has omitted the reference to the wife's adultery against
her husband. It may be argued, of course, that the latter is an addition by
Mark for the benefit of Roman audiences, which would have made no sense
in Palestine. And it could also be proposed that the addition of 'except for
unchastity' (corresponding to the variant in the other source followed by
Matthew in 5:32) is a concession made by the author(s) of Matthew to the
Jewish world in which they lived, or an acceptance by Matthew of the be-
liefs of that world, inasmuch as his adaptation of Mark would bring his
doctrine in line with a halakhah of the rabbinic School of Shammai. The
point about Roman and Palestinian audiences may have merit, and the
School of Shammai approach is hard to disprove (if we accept the view that
Jesus' basic ethical principles are deliberately distorted by Matthew), but
the evidence is at least equally respected if we suppose that here, as elsewhere, Matthew and Mark preserve separate versions of the same story.

Is any light on this shed by the other Synoptic passages on divorce
(Mt 5:32 and Lk 16:18)? According to Farmer Mt 5:32 is secondary in
the redactional history of Mark,[117] but this is mere speculation. Crouzel,
in a thorough survey of the patristic evidence, has recently argued that in
the period before Nicaea, it is Mt 5:32, not Mt 19:9 which is attested, and
goes on to argue that the 'texte primitif' of Mt 19:9 would be a repetition
of 5:32.[118] Now Matthew 5:32 also appears to contain a reference to unchastity as a ground for divorce, but it is concerned with a different issue,
that is, action by the man which makes his wife an adulteress (presumably
by virtually compelling her - given the social circumstances of the time - to
remarry). This passage of Matthew appears in the Sermon on the Mount,
and therefore derives from a different source or refers to a different

occasion in Jesus' career from that intended by 19:9. There is, of course, nothing in the least implausible about the idea that Jesus spoke of divorce on more than one occasion.

Butler, as we noted, held that Matthew 19:9 is secondary in the redactional history of Matthew; Crouzel's view need not imply that undemonstrable proposition. It only implies that the original text of 19:9 was in agreement with 5:32. The difficulty here might be why 19:9, in the form it commonly appears in modern editions, has such good manuscript support. To explain that we should have to assume that the original sense of the passage was not understood and that it was therefore corrected. What then is the intention of 5:32 (identical on this hypothesis with the original reading of 19:9)? Mt 5:32 is concerned with a man making his wife an adulteress by virtually compelling her to remarry. And what about the 'except on grounds of unchastity' clause? It may be suggested that this is merely a parenthesis. Jesus is not allowing 'divorce' for unchastity; he is merely alluding to the fact that if the separated wife is already guilty of unchastity she cannot be made an adulteress by her husband: she is one already.[119] Let us now suppose that this was the original sense of 19:9. Those who were familiar with the 'School of Shammai' tradition, failing to see Jesus' original intention, corrected the text at an early date, possibly in Egypt - thus ensuring its strong representation in the manuscript tradition. Thus a misunderstanding of the 'except for unchastity' clause leads to a mistaken reformulation of the whole saying, a reformulation which, as Butler saw, seems to contradict the sense of 19:3 - 8.

Let us now turn to Luke. Luke 16:18, though 'loose' in the 'Travel Narrative', and therefore presumably not directly dependent on Mark,[120] seems to contain a mixture of some of the ideas also found in Mark and in both passages of Matthew. It is not, however, concerned with making one's wife an adulteress (as at least is Mt 5:32), or with a wife divorcing her husband (as is Mark).[121] It repeats Mt 5:32 (but not Mark) about the adultery of the man who marries a divorcée.

All this adds up as follows:

(i) Luke is interested in the material in a different form from Matthew and Mark. He has two problems: *(a)* Can you divorce your wife and remarry? Answer: No; *(b)* Can you marry a divorcée? Answer: No.

(ii) Matthew has two accounts, both of which contain reference to 'unchastity' in connection with 'divorce'. Mt 5:32, but not 19:9 deals with marrying a divorcée.

(iii) Mark has an account roughly parallel to Mt 19:1ff., but different in details, some of which we have indicated.

The only reasonable conclusion which can be drawn from this material is that no evidence for any kind of direct literary descent should be extracted. The maximum permissible speculation should be that Luke 'adapts' Mark and Matthew, or the material available to them.

2. On temptations (Mt 18:6 - 9, Mk 9:42 - 8; cf. Lk 17:1 - 2)
Let us begin by noting that Luke is not in Markan context here and may safely be left aside. Concentrating then on Mark and Matthew and observing generally that each of them omits a certain part of the material the other provides, let us note in particular the following points:

(i) Mark glosses 'hell' in verse 44 as 'the unquenchable fire', thus adapting a tradition to a new type of reader.
(ii) Mark has 'to enter life ... to enter the kingdom of God' (verses 43, 45) where Matthew has 'to enter life' twice (verses 8, 9). According to Farmer this makes Mark 'secondary'.[122] This is possible, but 'secondary' is not the same as 'dependent'.
(iii) Mk 9:49 looks like an explanatory gloss. It does not occur in Matthew who runs on much more smoothly to 18:10 on the 'angels of little ones'.

It is evidence like that of point (iii) which might lead us to suppose that Matthew's sequence is original here and that if we are faced with literary derivation, it is more plausible to suppose that Mark has followed Matthew to the end of verse 9 and has then left him - but the break shows in his abrupt transition when compared with Matthew. But in fact Mt 18:10 does *not* follow particularly well after 18:9; it would come much more smoothly after Mt 18:6. So for different reasons neither Matthew nor Mark is particularly 'smooth' at this point.

Now on the theory of Markan priority we have to assume that Mt 18:7 derives from Q, represented also by Lk 17:1 in its different way. But it might be argued that Matthew (i.e., on this theory, Mark plus Q) is smoother than the original Mark, for Mt 18:7 at least provides a bridge over the jump in thought from Mk 9:42 to 9:43. It would be easier to argue that Mark has jerkily shortened the smoother text of Matthew.

But I should not wish to follow that road. What we have are two versions of the same material, in approximately, but not exactly equivalent contexts, with sufficient variation as to suggest likely independence of one another. We may note that another version of some of this material, combined with other ideas found in Mt 26:24, is presented by the early Clement of Rome.[123] Despite some of the editions I should not wish to argue Clement's dependence on any of our Gospel texts. Clement merely provides another example of the circulation of *logia* within the Christian communities.

3.   **Jesus and the sons of Zebedee** (Mt 20:20 - 8, Mk 10:35 - 45)
It seems clear beyond reasonable doubt that there is something wrong with Matthew's account - a phenomenon which we have noticed before, and which we have found hard to square with theories of literary derivation. In Matthew the request that James and John should sit at Jesus' right and left hand in his kingdom is made not by James and John themselves,[124] as in Mark, but by their mother. Now there is no reason thus far why Matthew's version may not be correct, but Matthew's narrative seems to assume, *after* the initial question, that the questioners were in fact James and John. For Jesus does not say (to the mother), 'Are *they* able to drink the cup that I am going to drink', but 'you [plural] do not know what you ask. Are *you* able to drink the cup which I am going to drink?' These words are virtually identical with what is presented by Mark. How then do we explain Matthew's version? Clumsy. Unless we opt again for *clumsy* bowdlerization, we have to posit a second source as well as Mark - if Matthew uses Mark at all - for the mother does not appear in Mark and it is most unlikely that Matthew simply invented her.[125] The most plausible explanation is that Matthew was aware of two features of the story: (1) that the question was posed not by James and John but by their mother; and (2) certain sentences of a widely known saying of Jesus. Whether Matthew or his source put these two elements together we do not know; what we do know is that dependence on Mark is a rather implausible explanation of the phenomenon observed and that Butler stretches the evidence too far in suggesting that Mark reproduces the 'substantial' truth in copying Matthew.[126] Admittedly Butler's view is more reasonable than its converse; it might be argued that either because a second source disagreed with Matthew, or because he realized that Matthew's version was not entirely coherent as it stands, Mark dropped all mention of the mother. And liturgical factors could account for an addition like verse 39. But such speculations are not particularly plausible.

4.   **Blind Bartimaeus** (Mt 20:29 - 34, Mk 10:46 - 52, Lk 18:35 - 43)
Both Mark and Matthew place this story immediately after the account of James and John (or their mother); Luke, who omits the story of the request, puts it after the third prediction of the Passion.[127] In other words all three Synoptics have the incident at the same point in the narrative. Of the three, however, only Mark has the name Bartimaeus, son of Timaeus. Matthew and Mark make the incident take place when Jesus is leaving Jericho, Luke as he approaches it. Mark, however, starts with the strange

sequence 'And *they* came to Jericho; and as *he* was leaving', which may
be merely 'simplified' in Luke. Perhaps more significant is that Matthew,
who does not name the blind man, in fact has two of them - possibly because at some stage the tradition supposed that Bartimaeus and the son of
Timaeus were different people. Yet we recall that in the story of the
Gadarene demoniacs (8:28 - 34) the 'doubling' phenomenon also occurs
in Matthew. However, it should be noted that Matthew has another story
about the healing of *two* blind men with certain parallels to this one ('Have
mercy on us, son of David') at 9:27ff., and this version, which apparently
does not derive from Mark, would seem to indicate a non-Markan tradition
about such a healing. As for Matthew's story at 20:29ff., we again notice
that (even apart from the omission of the name) it is more summary than
Mark's - a phenomenon which we have noticed a number of times already.
Nothing much can perhaps be shown from this, but we should at least notice that Matthew omits the significant 'Your faith has saved you' words
of Jesus which might seem worth preserving and which Luke preserves.
But, as so often, we have here an inconclusive *argumentum ex silentio*. All
that can properly be concluded is that if Matthew copied Mark he did (as
so often) a sloppy job, and if Mark copied Matthew he must have had very
good additional evidence to vary Matthew's story in the way that he has.
It should be observed that there is almost no additional material in Matthew
to suggest the hypothesis that Matthew combined Mark with Q.

5. The Entry into Jerusalem (Mt 21:1 - 9, Mk 11:1 - 10, Lk 19:28 - 38)
Perhaps the most interesting feature of this section, a portion of 'basic
Gospel' material which marks the beginning of the story of events at
Jerusalem in all three Synoptics, and which finds its parallel in John 12:
12 - 15, is that it highlights some of the strangeness of our text of Matthew.
Both Mark and Luke indicate that Jesus sent two of his disciples into a
village, telling them that they would find a colt there. In John's version
we read of a 'young ass' (ὀνάριον) . In Matthew, however, we find the
disciples instructed to bring an ass and a colt, that is, two animals, and the
insistence on two of them is carried so far that at verse 7 Jesus seems to be
seated on both of them.[128] The reason for this curiously clumsy version
is that Matthew wishes to cite Jesus' actions as the fulfilment of a prophecy of Zechariah, where he cites the words as 'riding on an ass and a
colt the foal of an ass' (ἐπιβεβηκὼς ἐπὶ ὄνον καὶ ἐπὶ πῶλον υἱὸν
ὑποζυγίου) .[129] John, however, who only finds it necessary for Jesus to
ride on one animal, cites the prophecy as 'sitting on the colt of an ass'
(καθήμενος ἐπὶ πῶλον ὄνου). It must be admitted, however, that John's
version of Zechariah is a mere paraphrase. In other words it looks as
though Matthew has varied the form of the incident to square with what

he took to be the sense of an Old Testament quotation, and has pushed this procedure to rather absurd lengths. I have argued at earlier stages of this discussion that apparently vague and imprecise material in Matthew can hardly be accounted for if he has a clear text of Mark in front of him; it is far more likely to have arisen in an oral tradition. It must be stated, however, that this is less likely to be a useful rule of thumb where an obvious reason for 'blurring' Mark might seem ready to hand - and in this case it is ready to hand, in a desire to square events with the prophecy of Zechariah which appeared to refer to two animals. Thus if Matthew had tampered with Mark *on this occasion* the result, though muddled and hardly liable to inspire the close modern reader with confidence, is at least intelligible. What we would then have is a deliberate perversion of historical record by Matthew. We should note that Luke omits the prophecy altogether, while John prefers to give a version of the prophecy which fits the likely facts, rather than the other way round.

But having said this much, we are still in no way nearer to knowing whether the confused version in Matthew arises from a perversion of *Mark,* or indeed what its precise genesis was. If it were abundantly clear that the rest of this story in Matthew depended on Mark, we could say that we had discovered a clear instance of the perversion of historical tradition in the interest of indicating the fulfilment of a prophecy; but we have not the evidence to say that. In general, as is common, Matthew's account is more summary than Mark's - possibly, though not inevitably, a sign of précis-making. But although much of the language of the two sections is similar, it is interesting to notice that in one part of the story where both Matthew and Mark provide full detail (both fuller than is available in Luke), their Greek is significantly different. Let us compare Mt 21:8 with Mk 11:8 and Lk 19:36:

Mt	Mk	Lk
ὁ δὲ πλεῖστος ὄχλος	καὶ πολλοὶ	πορευομένου δὲ
ἔστρωσαν ἑαυτῶν τὰ	τὰ ἱμάτια αὐτῶν	αὐτοῦ
ἱμάτια ἐν τῇ ὁδῷ,	ἔστρωσαν εἰς τὴν	ὑπεστρώννυον
ἄλλοι δὲ ἔκοπτον κλάδους	ὅδον, ἄλλοι δὲ	τὰ ἱμάτια αὐτῶν
ἀπὸ τῶν δένδρων καὶ	στιβάδας	ἐν τῇ ὁδῷ
ἐστρώννυον ἐν τῇ ὁδῷ	κόψαντες ἐκ τῶν ἀγρῶν	

In John's version, we should notice, there is no talk of putting palm-branches on the road, but of people carrying them in their hands, presumably waving them. Putting all this together, we can see that two actions occurred: some people took off their cloaks and spread them on the road, others did something or other with branches or foliage. According to John they waved palm-branches; according to Matthew they cut branches from the trees and spread them on the road; according to Mark they spread foliage (perhaps rushes) from the fields on to the road. Now if we are dealing with spreading things on the road, Mark's account looks better than Matthew's. στίβας is a more appropriate word. So it might look as though Mark's account is more authentic. But if Matthew is working from Mark, there is no reason whatever for him to vary στιβάδας ... ἐκ τῶν ἀγρῶν to κλάδους ἀπὸ τῶν δένδρων. In fact the Matthaean account, dealing with trees, looks more like a version of John's where it is specifically said that palm-branches are in question. It looks, in fact, as though Matthew knows the story about palm-trees (no idea of a palm-tree could be extracted from Mark and they may not in fact grow at the altitude of Jerusalem),[130] but *also* knows of another story according to which foliage was placed on the road along with the cloaks in Jesus' path. Luke avoids mentioning the vegetation altogether, so he provides no help. Yet leaving him aside we find that far from this section confirming any indication to be derived from the account of the two animals that Matthew depends on Mark, no sure corroboration is available; and indeed it appears *a priori* most unlikely. Could Mark have derived this story from Matthew? Perhaps the restoration of the one animal from two and the introduction of the more precise στιβάδας could be due to the checking of Matthew by a fresh witness, as Butler suggested, but this is not very convincing, and there is no particular reason why we should believe it to be the case. Yet there is certainly another sentence in Mark which has the authentic ring, but does not appear either in Matthew or in Luke: in Mark the crowds cry out (11:10) 'Blessed is the coming kingdom of our father David' - no doubt a genuinely revolutionary adaptation of the preceding quotation from Psalm 118:26 'Blessed is he who comes in the name of the Lord'. Now we are well aware that Matthew's versions of stories common to Mark and himself are often more abbreviated, but this omission is a striking one for a man generally admitted to be writing for a Jewish (and Jewish - Christian) audience. Again it is an argument *ex silentio,* but at least it does nothing to confirm Matthew's dependence on Mark. So it looks as though this section as a whole points in the usual direction: similarities, certainly, between Mark and Matthew, but the evidence is rather against literary dependence.

6. The Wicked Tenants (Mt 21:33 - 46, Mk 12:1 - 12, Lk 20:9 - 12)
Here we have another 'basic Gospel' story in the Triple Tradition, in the same place in each Gospel. There is a great deal of verbal parallelism in

each of the accounts - a prize case, it might appear, for proving literary dependence. Of course the section is a parable,[131] that is, it records words of Jesus, and we have already observed that it is a feature of the Synoptics that in such sections verbal parallelism is more likely. Let us, however, before assuming that this is a literary dependence passage, look at two sets of verbs. The first set deals with the killing of the heir. Is he killed before or after he is tossed out of the vineyard? The Greek is as follows:

Mt	Mk	Lk
λαβόντες	λαβόντες	—
ἐξέβαλον	ἀπέκτειναν	ἐκβαλόντες
ἀπέκτειναν	ἐξέβαλον	ἀπέκτειναν
i.e. he is killed	i.e. he is killed	i.e. he is killed
outside	inside	outside

So Matthew and Luke agree (perhaps in an older version of the incident, perhaps to provide an allegory for Jesus' death *outside* Jerusalem) against Mark.

Let us now look at the actions of the owner of the vineyard after the murder of the heir.

Mt	Mk	Lk
—	ἐλεύσεται	ἐλεύσεται
κακοὺς κακῶς ἀπολέσει	ἀπολέσει	ἀπολέσει
ἐκδώσεται	δώσει ˙	δώσει

In this case we have a classic example of the exact agreement of Mark and Luke against Matthew, giving evidence, perhaps, in favour of literary dependence between Mark and Luke. Matthew is the odd man out; his version is substantially different in that it introduces a literary conceit (κακοὺς κακῶς) which represents nothing in Mark.

If we put these two passages together we find, in small but significant ways, Matthew varying from Mark, once being closer (in thought) to Luke, while in the other instance diverging from both. So these variants in the tradition of a passage with marked general similarities indicate a tendency in Matthew to represent something a little different. Of course, it might be added that there are sections even of this narrative which Matthew has but Mark does not, and vice versa, but these could perhaps be suspected as later additions. I am thinking particularly of Mt 21:43: 'Therefore I tell you, the kingdom of God will be taken away from you and given to a people producing its fruits'. Those who argue for the dependence of Matthew on Mark can (as often) fall back on interpolation to rid themselves of this one.

7. The Abomination of Desolation (Mt 24:15 - 22, Mk 13:14 - 20, Lk 21:20 - 4)

It is impossible to avoid saying something about this notoriously troublesome section of the Synoptic Apocalypse, but my remarks must be limited and tentative. It is clear that, although all three Synoptics put the Apocalypse as a whole and the section about the 'Abomination of Desolation' in particular in the same place in their narratives, in the 'Abomination' sections Matthew and Mark are substantially different from Luke. Both Mark and Matthew speak of the 'abomination of desolation' while Luke says that 'desolation' will be recognized as approaching when Jerusalem is invested by armies. Many commentators, supposing that Luke is adapting a *post eventum* prophecy to the actual circumstances of the siege of Jerusalem by Titus, and supposing him to be writing his Gospel after Jerusalem's fall, argue that he has substituted - a deliberate fraud - a historical fact for a 'mere' Old Testament prophecy. The whole section (and particularly verses 20 and 24) is even used as strong evidence for the dating of Luke after A.D.70. But even assuming that Luke is prophesying *post eventum* the latter point is not demonstrated, for from the mid-sixties many in Palestine could have recognized that the writing was on the wall. Be that as it may, we probably have a different tradition in Luke, who in speaking of 'the days of vengeance', echoes Deuteronomy 32:35 in a way which Matthew would not easily have passed over had he known of it.

So we may consider the relation of Mark and Matthew without troubling with Luke at this point. And it is clear that they are very close to one another verbally. Apart from the actual words of Jesus - which we have generally regarded as more likely to be preserved precisely whether the tradition is oral or written - we find that even the parenthetical note to the reader (ὁ ἀναγινώσκων νοείτω) occurs both times. The difference is in the exact words dealing with the 'abomination', for while Matthew refers to it 'standing (ἑστός) in the holy place' (quoting Daniel whom he mentions by name), Mark provides us (apparently) with 'standing where it ought not', with the syntactically curious form ἑστήκοτα. Mark's version is probably somehow corrupt, but it is difficult merely to identify the original with what we find in Matthew. For apart from the fact that Matthew is more likely to have added the longer reference to Daniel, Mark could hardly have written as he has if he had Matthew in front of him.

Probably behind our Mark and Matthew lie earlier variants in the tradition. But if there were such variants, they presumably contained references to the 'holy place', for at least two traditions must have included the cautionary phrase 'let the reader understand'. But although that is a bold claim - requiring this time a *written* tradition pre-dating Mark and Matthew - it is not unacceptable in the special case of the Abomination of Desolation.

But why should we not simply say that Matthew copied Mark, adding in the reference to Daniel (and to the Sabbath in verse 20)? If it seemed likely that this was Matthew's procedure in the remainder of chapters 24 and 25, that conclusion would be necessary. But we shall shortly see that Matthew's procedure is quite different.

8.   The end of the Parousia section (Mt 24:34 - 25:46)

Mark's account of the Parousia ends at 13:37, but he departs from close parallelism with Matthew (and Luke) at 13:32. The last sentence where Mark and Matthew run in tandem is the striking 'But of that day and hour no one knows, not even the angels of heaven, nor the Son, but the Father only'.[132] The sentence looks like a culmination, and Mark merely follows it with an exhortation to be watchful.

Matthew also has a theme of watching, but develops it greatly with other material, much of which is found elsewhere in Luke, but in different contexts, but some of which - and above all the passage on the Last Judgment with which Matthew concludes chapter 25 - is found in Matthew alone. Clearly this material was floating in the tradition, and Matthew, following his usual pattern, fitted it in here, where he found it appropriate. So it might appear at first sight as though Matthew followed Mark as far as Mark went, and then added in his extra material. *But in fact this is not what Matthew has done.* For Matthew does not include Mk 13:33 - 7 in Mark's place, but scatters versions of it through the remainder of his chapters 24 and 25 (cf. Mt 24:42, 25:14 - 15, 25:13). In fact it seems as though Matthew has versions of this particular 'Markan' material available, but from (and in) a source other than Mark. What has happened in chapters 24 and 25 is that Mark and the Matthew-source have overlapped, but there is no reason to suppose that the Matthew-source is Mark. In fact since the 'Markan' sections are fitted excellently into non-Markan contexts, there is every reason to suppose that the Matthew-source is not Mark.[133] So it is clear that Matthew does not use Mk 13:33 - 7 as his source, and since this leads on well enough after Mark 13:32, it is reasonable to suppose that although Mk 13:30 - 2 parallels Matthew 24:34 - 6, Mark is not the source of Matthew at this point either.

What about the other alternative? Butler thinks that in Mk 13:33 - 7 Mark has merely 'telescoped' Matthew, and his general explanation of the end of the Parousia section is that since everything in Mark can be found in some sixty-one verses of Matthew, we are driven to the conclusion that Mark must be dependent. But this explanation of Mark assumes in Mark at this point an incompetence which we have hitherto only identified in Matthew, if the Two-Documentarians are correct. On Butler's thesis Mark has simply assimilated the Thief in the Night (Mt 24:42 - 4) with the parable of the Absent Master and the Talents.[134]

Finally we may note that if the words 'nor the Son' are missing from Mt 24:36, then Mark could not have got them from that source. But the text, as we indicated earlier, is so uncertain that nothing can be proved from it.

9. The Anointing at Bethany (Mt 26:6 - 13, Mk 14:3 - 9; cf. Lk 7:36 - 50, Jn 12:1 - 8)

Matthew and Mark agree in their positioning in the narrative of a story of the anointing of Jesus by a woman at the house of Simon the leper. In other ways too, their versions are close, but with minor variants of interest. John has a somewhat similar story, which he too places in Bethany, but just before the triumphal entry into Jerusalem. But John identifies the woman as Mary, sister of Martha and Lazarus, and *seems* to suppose that the anointing occurred at their house. Luke's version, which is clearly derived from a source other than Mark or Matthew, places the incident in Galilee, though also at the house of a man called Simon. But this time Simon is a Pharisee and the 'woman', who is not named, is identified as a 'sinner', presumably therefore as a prostitute. John's version seems to take over something from Luke's, such as the fact that the woman (or Mary) wiped Jesus' feet with her hair, a detail missing in Mark and Matthew. On the other hand John associates the incident (as do Mark and Matthew) with the coming burial of Jesus, while Luke puts it in the context of the forgiveness of sins. John says that it was Judas Iscariot who complained of Mary's behaviour ('because he was a thief'), Matthew says that it was 'the disciples', Mark more generally that there were complaints, while Luke offers something quite different. For while the others complain that the value of the ointment could have been given to the poor, in Luke the (unvoiced) concern of Simon is that Jesus did not recognize that he was being touched by a prostitute. Finally we should observe that John and Mark share the strange description of the ointment as νάρδου πιστικῆς. [135] All in all the relationships of all the versions are inordinately complicated.

Fortunately it is not our present concern to unravel them all. What we want is a comparison of the two versions, which in every relevant respect are very close indeed. They are even very close verbally, and thus provide interest where they differ in details of wording. Let us list some differences in parallel columns, forgetting about differences merely in the order of words.

Mt	Mk
ἀνακειμένου	κατακειμένου
μύρου βαρυτίμου	μύρου νάρδου πιστικῆς πολυτέλους
κατέχεεν ἐπὶ τῆς κεφαλῆς	κατέχεεν . . . τῆς κεφαλῆς
οἱ μαθηταὶ ἠγανάκτησαν	ἦσαν . . . τινες ἀγανακτοῦντες
πραθῆναι πολλοῦ	πραθῆναι ἐπάνω δηναρίων τριακοσίων
—	ἐνεβριμῶντο αὐτῇ
βαλοῦσα . . . αὕτη τὸ μύρον	προσέλαβεν μυρίσαι τὸ σῶμα
τοῦτο ἐπὶ τοῦ σώματος	
πρὸς τὸ ἐνταφιάσαι	εἰς τὸν ἐνταφιασμόν
ἐν ὅλῳ τῷ κόσμῳ	εἰς ὅλον τὸν κόσμον

Matthew omits the exact sum of money, and drops the second of the pair ἀγανακτοῦντες . . . ἐνεβριμῶντο, but in general the impression of the two passages is of two very similar accounts but with strangely different linguistic forms. There seems to be no reason to suppose that either Mark or Matthew here has *corrected* a clearly available written text, or has tidied up the grammar. What seems far more likely is that they present slightly different versions of the same account, which, for fairly obvious reasons, had been preserved with a good deal of care. There is another line of approach; they are two slightly different Greek versions of an original Aramaic text. There is no question but that Mark's Gospel was originally written in Greek, though the tradition behind it is clearly at least in part Aramaic. There is, of course, a tradition that Matthew was originally in Aramaic, so there is a possibility that our versions of Mark and Matthew are both versions of an earlier Aramaic Matthew. But it is not *necessary* to take up that solution. Even if our Matthew is a translation of an Aramaic Matthew, it need not be the case that Mark derives directly from any such Aramaic document. At least equally likely is the theory that he derives from a well-formed Aramaic tradition. The very close similarity between our texts of Mark and Matthew might well suggest some form of common origin.

10. Preparing the Passover (Mt 26:17 - 19, Mk 14:12 - 16, Lk 22:7 - 13)
As a contrast to the rather sloppily organized Parousia section of Mark, we have here one of the sections where Matthew's version seems to be not only abbreviated, but sloppy in comparison with Mark and Luke. There

are a number of verbal similarities, and Mark and Luke are in fact very close throughout. A striking omission in Matthew, however, is that whereas both Mark and Luke have Jesus tell two of his disciples (Peter and John in Luke) to go into the city where they will meet a man doing the womanly job of carrying a jug of water on his head, Matthew simply says that they will meet 'someone' (τὸν δεῖνα). It is again hard to conceive of this vague and inadequate version being dependent on the account in Mark. (Nor, of course, could Mark have got his version from Matthew. If he corrected Matthew, it was by a version so superior that he should have followed it throughout.) That Matthew's source is in fact different from Mark even in this Triple Tradition passage is confirmed by the variations in the next sentence:

Mt   'My time is near: I will keep the Passover at your house with my disciples'.

Mk   'Where is my room where I am to eat the Passover with the disciples?'

Lk   'Where is the room where I am to eat the Passover with my disciples?'

In short, we have seen this sort of 'summary' passage of Matthew before; Matthew gives us a resumé of traditional material which is not an abbreviation of Mark.

11.   The Institution (Mt 26:26 - 9, Mk 14:22 - 5, Lk 22:15 - 20; cf. I Cor. 11:25)

These notoriously difficult passages are worth brief comment here because this is one of the few places where 'liturgical' influence on the text of Matthew and Mark is likely. If we compare their versions with Paul's in Corinthians we notice substantial differences. Perhaps the most significant of these are: (1) in Paul the cup is taken 'after supper', while in the Synoptics (more 'ritually') the bread and the cup follow one another; and (2) Matthew and Mark do not have Paul's 'Do this in remembrance of me.' In this second case it is Paul's version which looks the more liturgical. So we have to assume that very early on slightly different versions were in circulation (Luke's is different again). But if these early versions were somewhat influenced by ritual use, that argues against Matthew taking his from Mark or vice versa. Such dependence becomes merely one of very many possibilities.[136]

12.   The arrest of Jesus

Generally speaking Mt 26:45 - 50 is very close verbally to Mk 14:41 - 6; Luke, telling the same story, is much more remote.[137] But after verse 50 Matthew's account is much the more elaborate, and he adds in various comments of Jesus' arising out of the servant of the High Priest having his ear cut off. Literary dependence is obviously possible in the earlier section, but if so, why does Matthew abandon Mark at verse 51 or Mark Matthew after verse 46? Mark is indeed unlikely to be following Matthew here; he omits what seem crucial words of Jesus and what he says is very brief and non-Matthaean in language. Of course, it could be claimed that Matthew's original text has been tampered with, but that claim is always open to anyone who wants to show that 'really' Mark and Matthew present similar material - and it should be treated accordingly. But could not Matthew have followed Mark until he reached 14:46 and then abandoned him for a fuller source? That is certainly possible, and necessarily the case if one assumes that literary dependence is the only way of explaining Mt 26:45 - 50 as against Mk 14:41 - 6.

As for the young man in the linen cloak who was arrested and fled naked (according to Mark), that appears neither in Luke nor in Matthew. But there is no particular reason why it should. The detail is obviously important for some reason to Mark (perhaps, as they say, it was Mark), but it is not important to the narrative. Of course Morton Smith thinks the young man was being baptized, and that since baptism was part of Jesus' secret teaching, Matthew and Luke suppressed it.[138] But if that is true, not only Matthew and Luke, but Mark also, give a totally dishonest account of the events in the Garden prior to Jesus' arrest. It is only because people wore linen cloths for baptism that Smith thinks the young man was being baptized. (Everyone who wears a uniform is a soldier because soldiers wear uniforms!)

13. The death sentence (Mt 27:15 - 26, Mk 15:6 - 15)
It might perhaps be argued that in his account of Jesus before the Sanhedrin Matthew preserves relics of a different (and more authentic) tradition than Mark, for in one or two minor particulars he seems farther from the apparently false picture found in Luke that there was an official trial in a morning-session of the Sanhedrin in the council chamber. The correct account of these transactions seems to be that an unofficial gathering of some members of the Sanhedrin took place at night at the house of the High Priest (or at the house of Ananas), an illegal time and place for a properly constituted meeting. Jesus was judged to deserve death and at a second session in the morning it was decided to denounce him to the Romans and make sure that the killing was handled by Pilate.[139] In Mark, in contrast with Matthew, there is twice mention of the *whole* council being present (14:53, 15:1) and 15:1 comes near to suggesting a formal meeting; it must be admitted, however, that Matthew does refer to the whole council at 26:59 (= Mk 14:55). Secondly Mark seems to get rather nearer the notion of a formal condemnation (κατέκριναν) at 14:64 than does Matthew

in the corresponding section (26:66), though his parallel use of ἔνοχος
may merely indicate that Jesus was judged *worthy* of death rather than
condemned to death.

Final decisions on these matters are difficult, and certainty may be impossible to attain, but the section on the death sentence has a certain interest that deserves special consideration in that it encapsulates a number of
the problems we have already met many times. It could be argued that
Matthew's version, which is fuller than Mark's, is an expansion of Mark, i.e.
Mark plus further material (such as Pilate's wife's dream and Pilate's hand-
washing).[140] Or it could be said that Mark is a contraction of Matthew.
Both these are possible, equally so. The significant point is that all that is
really evident in the passages is that they both recount the same events,
frequently in the same words. But that in itself proves nothing about priority. And we should notice that there must be some explanation of the
fact that when Mark and Matthew 'coincide' there is no pattern established
in the manner of treatment of one Gospel by the other - if one is in fact
dependent on the other.

14. The Cry of Desolation (Mt 27:46, Mk 15:34)
The weight of manuscript evidence seems to indicate that Matthew preserved the cry 'My God' in-Hebrew, though the original *word* must have
been 'Eliya', easily confused with 'Elijah'. Mark seems to have preferred
the Aramaic, which cannot be correct and could not be so confused.[141]
If this is the case, we have a clear example of a passage where Matthew's
version is the more reliable, and where it is most unlikely that either
Matthew or Mark (as distinct from the later copyists of their texts) followed the version supplied by the other. If Matthew corrected Mark, why
did he correct one word into Hebrew and leave the rest in Aramaic? Perhaps the Hebrew of Codex Bezae is the original Matthew.[142]

15. Joseph of Arimathea (Mt 27:57 - 61, Mk 15:42 - 7)
This time Matthew's account is the more abbreviated, but it *could* be précis;
Mark's is fuller and it *could* be expansion. But why either? And we should
note that Matthew omits the seemingly significant fact that Joseph was a
member of the council (repeated by Luke), and that contrary to Mark and
Luke Matthew says that the tomb was 'his own'.

The intent of this chapter has been to argue that in the latter sections
of Mark and Matthew, and even in the Passion Narrative where pressure to
fix a common sequence and to determine common vocabulary for trans-
mitting the story of Jesus must have been particularly strong, we find the
same phenomena as we found in the earlier sections of the Gospels. Our
survey has been incomplete, but enough has been compiled to enable

conclusions to be drawn with an acceptable degree of accuracy. It only remains, before we attempt to identify our conclusions, to see what happens to Matthew (and Luke) at the end of Mark; for we began by considering the situation in the other Synoptics at the point where the text of Mark begins.

8

THE END OF MARK

All commentators on Mark have recognized the peculiar problem of the ending. It is generally recognized that what may within limits be called authentic Mark comes to an end at 16:8 with the words 'for they were afraid' ($\dot{\epsilon}\phi o\beta o\tilde{\upsilon}\nu\tau o$ $\gamma\dot{\alpha}\rho$), and that the so-called longer and shorter endings are compilations based largely on other Gospel accounts.[143] Scholars have therefore attempted to determine whether Mark really did end in such an abrupt fashion, or whether the original ending has been lost. Of course an abrupt ending could be the sign not of Mark's intention but of his death for some reason or other before his work was complete or, as Streeter suggested, of the destruction of the last pages of the original copy. In any event, since it seems certain that $\dot{\epsilon}\phi o\beta o\tilde{\upsilon}\nu\tau o$ $\gamma\dot{\alpha}\rho$ were, from a very early period indeed, the last genuine words of Mark available, it would be of considerable interest if the character of the narrative in Matthew (or Luke) changed at this point. Luke, in fact, provides very little help, though it does give us one curiosity which may be of interest. For Matthew is much closer to Mark than Luke at this point, and Luke seems to be following a non-Markan emphasis of Resurrection appearances in Jerusalem rather than in Galilee; Luke (24:6) gives us the words of the angels (plural) as 'Remember how he told you while he was still in Galilee'. Matthew and Mark, in a variant tradition, have the angel (singular) say that Jesus 'is going before you into Galilee', and that 'you will see him' there. So we can leave Luke aside.

Concentrating on the relationship between Mark and Matthew, however, we should notice that the divergence should be said to begin not with the last words of Mark at 16:8, but with the end of 16:7. It is of course true that even if Matthew is following Mark from 28:1 on, he is filling Mark out by another (and more miracle-laden) source, the source of the 'great earthquake' in 28:2. But somehow or other, and despite this, as we have seen, the words of the angel are very similar in both accounts, so the *possibility* of literary dependence remains. But let us now compare Mt 28:8 with Mk 16:8.

Mt	Mk
καὶ ἀπελθοῦσαι ταχὺ ἀπὸ τοῦ	καὶ ἐξελθοῦσαι ἔφυγον ἀπὸ τοῦ
μνημείου μετὰ φόβου καὶ χαρᾶς	μνημείου, εἶχεν γὰρ αὐτὰς τρόμος
μεγάλης ἔδραμον ἀπαγγεῖλαι	καὶ ἔκστασις. καὶ οὐδενὶ
τοῖς μαθηταῖς αὐτοῦ	οὐδὲν εἶπαν, ἐφοβοῦντο γάρ

In Matthew the women run to tell the disciples what they have seen; in Mark apparently they say nothing. Yet this cannot be what Mark originally intended to express. At the very least Mark must have intended to say something to the effect that 'they said nothing to anyone, *but* they went to find Simon Peter', as John more or less gives the story. In other words our Mark *must* be incomplete, so that it is possible that Matthew's line 'they ran to tell the disciples' is *either* a version of an original longer Mark *or* an expansion of a Mark he found (or even recognized to be) incomplete. But if Matthew knew a longer Mark, we should enquire about the material in Matthew after 28:8. What is this remaining material? First there is a story of Jesus meeting the women, which looks like a version of the account in John of the meeting with Mary Magdalene. In other words Matthew has tacked on a Magdalene story to the story of the woman at the tomb which he took (on this theory) from Mark. The assumption in the theory of Matthew knowing a longer Mark would have to be, therefore, that Mark originally told his tale in the form: (1) Mary Magdalene and the other women meet the angel, are terrified, and say nothing (despite the injunction to 'tell the disciples and Peter'); (2) they meet Jesus and *then* speak of their experiences to the other disciples. But if this was all in Mark, then not only did Matthew produce a garbled version of it, but Luke omitted one important fact altogether - the fact that Mary Magdalene and the other women saw Jesus.[144] For that is not given, though the vision of the angels is given; Luke's account is at 24:22 - 3. All this points to the conclusion that neither Matthew nor Luke knew a longer text of Mark.

The other possibility - if we assume the use of Mark by Matthew - is that Matthew turned to another source after he had reached the Markan ἐφοβοῦντο γάρ. This 'other source' would presumably be the same one that he used for the earlier part of chapter 28; indeed it might just as well be the case that Matthew used that 'source' throughout the whole of chapter 28. But let us ignore this and consider whether Matthew used Mark where possible up to ἐφοβοῦντο γάρ and then, perforce, went elsewhere. What do the remaining sections of Matthew consist in? Do they necessitate the conclusion that Matthew flounders when he reaches the end of Mark because he has no other good source available? Indeed they do not. They

are, in fact, three sections, and it will be advisable to consider each briefly
in turn:

    (i) Mt 28:9 - 10. As we have seen, this is another Magdalene
       story, probably paralleled in John and confirmatory of
       the advice of the angel. I have previously suggested that the
       appearance to Mary was probably not in the text of Mark as
       known to Matthew or Luke, but it fits perfectly well into
       the Matthaean narrative. In other words there is no jarring
       change of gears after Matthew 28:8.[145]
   (ii) Mt 28:11 - 15. This story of the bribing of the soldiers picks
       up Mt 27:62 - 6 and presumably comes from the same source.[146]
       But it flows on smoothly enough from what has immediately
       preceded it and could have followed similarly in an earlier
       setting. At any rate it is clear that Matthew has substantial
       sources continuing beyond the point where Mark breaks off,
       and this section is appropriately placed to round off an
       incident which had occurred earlier.
  (iii) Mt 28:16 - 20. These last verses complete the narrative
       without leaving any loose ends, though somewhat abruptly.
       The Eleven proceed to Galilee, see Jesus there and are com-
       manded to go out and preach. It is true that this looks as
       though it could have been added by almost anyone on the
       basis of the narrative up to 28:15, but since the narrative up
       to 28:15 does not argue for Matthew being in trouble or
       forced to abrupt changes of tactic at the end of Mark, nothing
       can be deduced from this.

We may conclude that the section of Matthew's text that follows the
end of Mark points, if anywhere, to the fact that Matthew is not dependent on Mark for his accounts of the empty tomb and its sequels.

9

SUMMARY AND PROSPECTS

It is time to take stock. We have examined a great number of passages in the Synoptic Gospels, some from the so-called Triple Tradition, some from the basic Gospel framework that we identified in Chapter One, and many others besides. We have pointed to the difficulties involved in showing particular passages, let alone particular Gospels, as more primitive, and we have observed that even if in a particular passage it can be shown that either Matthew or Mark is the more primitive, it does not follow that he is necessarily also the older, let alone the source, of his more sophisticated parallel text. We have argued that in many places it is certainly incorrect to infer derivation from close similarities of wording.

It is also necessary to draw attention to a fact so obvious that it has been regularly overlooked. If we ask the question; 'Did Jesus ever say the same thing twice, or even three times, in more or less the same words?', we can only answer, 'What preacher doesn't?' So we should be surprised if we did *not* find in the Gospels very similar passages, regardless of whether or not we subscribe to a theory of literary dependence. And we might expect to find amalgamated versions of oft-told parables, and similar verbalizations of similar preaching in different places.

We have observed a number of occasions where now Mark, now Matthew, gives expanded versions of similar themes, Matthew being fuller particularly in his descriptions of the earlier part of Jesus' ministry and in parts of the Parousia and Passion narratives.[147] Bearing this in mind we wonder what answer can reasonably be given to the question, 'Who expands whom?' And we have noticed on a number of occasions (e.g. the Death of John the Baptist, Jairus' Daughter, Blind Bartimaeus, etc.) that if Matthew is copying, or working from a written Mark, he is at times unbelievably careless, and that no easy explanations such as theological concern serve to explain this away - especially as elsewhere he seems perfectly capable of doing the job properly, particularly in many of the 'basic Gospel sections'. And again we have argued that in many 'Markan' passages Matthew uses a non-Markan source, so that after a while it becomes legitimate to ask the upholders of Markan priority whether this source has become so wide, as in the passages dealing with the Confession at Caesarea Philippi, as to cause trouble for the whole hypothesis of derivation from Mark.

In our opening chapter we pointed to the major methodological difficulty into which almost all contemporary writers on the Synoptic Problem seem to have fallen, the problem of assuming that if Mark is not dependent on Matthew, then Matthew is dependent on Mark, or vice versa. In avoiding this trap I do not wish to assert that there are no passages where it may well be the case that Mark looks the older and where Matthew may be dependent, or that there are no passages where the converse seems to be a plausible explanation. Nor do I recommend neglecting such facts as that Matthew and Luke very rarely agree in order against Mark. In order to meet these points and to account for the familiar arguments about the nature of the various Synoptic materials, it seems that we should set out an argument as follows:

(1)   A certain amount of evidence seems to suggest that Mark is prior to Matthew.

(2)   A certain amount of evidence seems to suggest that Matthew is prior to Mark.

From this two possibilities seem to follow:

(1)   *If* one Gospel is the source of the other, Mark is the source of Matthew.

(2)   *If* one Gospel is the source of the other, Matthew is the source of Mark.

For these two possibilities three alternative explanations seem to be available:

(1)   Matthew and Mark both depend on a common written source.

(2)   Neither Gospel is the literary source of the other.

(3)   There is a mutual contamination of original Mark by Matthew and of original Matthew by Mark.

We shall have to consider each of these alternatives.

Alternative (3), the theory of mutual contamination, seems to be growing in popularity, and has been explicitly recommended by Sanders.[148] It has the advantage of being able to account for the contradictory evidence about whether Matthew or Mark is prior, without abandoning the basic assumptions about the literary dependence of Gospel texts. But its disadvantages must not be overlooked. It entails an Ur-Markus as well as an Ur-Matthäus, and the contents of these hypothetical Gospels must remain largely unverifiable. Now it is true, as we shall see, that there is an ancient

tradition about the existence of a Proto-Matthew, but attempts to identify
an Ur-Markus have found no patristic support. We should note further
that even if Morton Smith's new Secret Gospel of Mark were to be proved
authentic, it would not fit the bill, for the Secret Gospel is supposed to be
an expansion, not a simpler version, of canonical Mark. It must be stated
that there is no way in which we can go back behind the simple and direct
narrative of canonical Mark to any hypothetical predecessor supposedly
free of Matthaean contamination. And we may reasonably say that although the existence of such an earlier version is remotely possible, it
seems to be most unlikely. As an hypothesis, therefore, it should be dis-
carded if anything more plausible can be proposed.

Let us now consider alternative (1), the thesis that both Mark and
Matthew depend on some common literary source. Although the possible
nature of such a source admits of very wide variations, in practice we
should limit ourselves to two forms of the only seriously proposed version.
If there is a common literary source, scholars have supposed that it is either
to be identified with an early Aramaic Gospel of Matthew, or with perhaps
other material in the form of notes originally compiled by Matthew, but
not strictly to be equated with what we should allow to deserve the name
Gospel.

Scholars who believe that canonical Matthew and Mark both depend on
an Aramaic document normally operate with one of two models as follows:

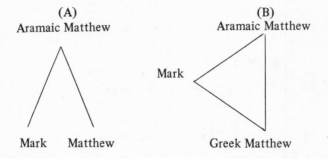

I propose to leave model (A) aside for the time being and look at (B), which
allows its supporters to maintain the priority of Aramaic Matthew while
still accepting that the author of Greek Matthew is influenced by Mark. It
is important to notice that this proposal, which accepts the evidence of
Papias of Hierapolis that Matthew wrote a Gospel in Aramaic (or just possibly Hebrew),[149] assumes, as Papias does not, that the Aramaic Matthew
is earlier than Mark. Furthermore it must be taken to assert that our Mark
is dependent on a Matthew very substantially different from canonical

Matthew. For if this were not so, we should be making Mark depend on Matthew in all those passages where we have argued that such dependence is unlikely or impossible. Nevertheless many scholars have been prepared to accept this situation, because it allows them to hold both that something like canonical Matthew is the earliest Gospel, and that canonical Mark is older than canonical Matthew. We have argued that this latter proposition is unproven, but we must admit at once that there is one rather striking set of facts, not much used by Markan priorists, that provides perhaps the strongest argument for model (B) or some other version of Markan priority to canonical Matthew. The facts are best set out by Gundry,[150] and are essentially as follows: if we look at the Old Testament quotations and allusions in canonical Matthew, we find that whereas in non-Markan passages there is no sign of the dominance of either the Septuagint or the Hebrew Bible as a source of quotations, and in *allusions* to the Old Testament in Markan passages this pattern is repeated, the pattern is completely different in 'formal quotations' common to Mark and Matthew. In these formal quotations, to quote Gundry, 'The Marcan formal quotations are almost purely Septuagintal and the Matthaean parallels a little less so.'[151]

Gundry has pointed out two features of the Synoptic tradition: that, in his opinion, a formal Gospel written in Aramaic (or Hebrew) cannot account for the Septuagintal element deeply embedded in the Synoptics; and that the argument from common formal quotations necessitates the dependence of canonical Matthew on Mark.[152] With the first of these points we need not concern ourselves at present. We shall approach it again when we consider the possible nature of a pre-canonical Semitic source. Our immediate concern is with the argument from formal quotations. In Gundry's view there is no alternative but the use of Mark by canonical Matthew. But that implies that the author of Greek Matthew had the whole of Mark available, and the consequences of that are that the author of Greek Matthew has produced varying degrees of chaos in certain sections that appear in Mark in a tidy and organized form, such as the Death of John the Baptist or the Rich Young Man, or the Sons of Zebedee or the events of Palm Sunday. A hypothesis that has to tolerate such results does not readily command assent, particularly in view of our collection of evidence that Matthew and Mark are probably independent of one another. But what of the formal quotations? Is another explanation possible? Two alternatives, separately or in combination, may be mentioned. On the one hand the text of Matthew, in common formal quotations, may have been assimilated to that of Mark. The difficulty with that is that no variations appear in the textual tradition of Matthew, whereas we might expect substantial variations if such a process of assimilation had occurred. The other alternative is that in the relevant sections of Mark and Matthew the original versions of the tradition were in the Septuagintal version. The difficulty with that might seem to be that the coincidence is remarkable. A mixture of these two explanations lessens these difficulties, but by no means eliminates them. There is, however, a slightly different possibility available: that the Septuagintalisms in Matthew are original, while in formal quotations Mark is simply Septuagintal throughout. If we adopt this explanation, there is no coincidence in finding Mark Septuagintal in one area where Matthew is, i.e. in common formal quotations, for Mark is Septuagintal in *all* formal quotations. I would submit that this is in fact the most likely hypothesis for, as Gundry says, 'the formal quotations in Mark are almost purely Septuagintal - often slavishly so.'[153] Confirmation of it may be found in the fact that if our argument (following Streeter) is correct, our texts of Mark all depend on one defective copy. Now if this copy were originally Septuagintal in formal quotations or were corrected into a Septuagintal form, all our texts of Mark would be Septuagintal in this area.[154] Then if in the formal quotations common to Mark and Matthew we found an overwhelming predominance of Septuagintal forms we should only have to assume that in these places the Matthaean tradition was Septuagintal. And that need not be in the least surprising.

Keeping still within the limits of our alternative (1), the thesis that canonical Mark and Matthew both depend on a common literary source, we must now restrict ourselves to model (A) above. According to this model, canonical Mark and Matthew both depend on an Aramaic Matthew. It is important to distinguish this theory from the more obviously acceptable accounts which say that there are strong traditions in Semitic sources lying behind our canonical Gospels of Mark and Matthew. We shall not discuss these traditions and their nature until a little later. What we must do now is to attempt to isolate the evidence for a specifically Aramaic *Gospel* earlier than our Matthew which could be a literary source for both Matthew and Mark.

The earliest, as well as the most controversial evidence for what seems to be an Aramaic Gospel is the notorious text of Papias:[155] 'Matthew composed [arranged?] the *logia* in a language used by the Jews, and everyone interpreted them as well as he could'. 'A language used by the Jews'[156] probably refers to Aramaic, and perhaps the first point we should note is that Papias does not refer to any kind of authorized translation. Papias, of course, thinks that the 'Aramaic' *logia* were composed by the apostle, but his evidence does not point to a belief that the original Aramaic Matthew was rendered into Greek by Matthew; it may rather indicate that he thought that it was not. On the interpretation of the word *logia* itself, it seems that Papias really did intend a Gospel in the strict sense of the word. In telling us that Mark did not produce a complete account (σύνταξιν) of the *logia* of the Lord, he seems clearly to equate *logia* with an account of 'things said or done by the Lord'.[157]

Unfortunately this text of Papias is almost all the early evidence we have to go on. The only other possible help in the first two centuries is Irenaeus, who tells us that Matthew wrote his Gospel 'among the Jews in their own language at the time when Peter and Paul were evangelizing in Rome and laying the foundations of the Church.'[158] This passage might seem to offer a clear date for Matthew's Gospel in Aramaic, viz. the sixties of the first century, which we suggested in Chapter One was a quite plausible time for Matthew, but we cannot discount the possibility that Irenaeus is himself only relying on Papias for his information. And we should also note that if Matthew is a source for Luke, it seems that it must be Matthew in its canonical form, that is, in Greek. That would mean that the Aramaic version would have to be pushed back even earlier.

It seems clear that in the fourth century A.D., and presumably long before, a work known as the Gospel of the Nazaraeans was widely thought to derive from Matthew and to be written in a Semitic language. The earliest evidence for this Gospel is probably Hegesippus (*c.* 180), but the comment which best illuminates our present problem was made by Jerome in chapter three of his *De Viris Illustribus*:[159]

Jerome writes as follows:
'Matthew in Judaea was the first to compose the gospel of Christ in the Hebrew character and speech for the sake of those who came over to the faith from Judaism; who he was who later translated it into Greek is no longer known with certainty. Further the Hebrew text itself is still preserved in the library at Caesarea which the martyr Pamphilus collected with great care. The Nazaraeans in Beroea, a city of Syria, who use this book, also permitted me to copy it.'

This passage clearly indicates that Jerome is talking about a Gospel which he admits derives (as he thinks) from Matthew, but which is not a Semitic version of our Matthew. Jerome is not very familiar with it (he says he copied it in Beroea), and since the work was to be found in the library at Caesarea, it is almost certainly to be identified with a Gospel referred to by Eusebius as follows: 'Since the Gospel that has come down to us in the Hebrew script turns the threat not against him ... I put myself the question whether according to Matthew ...'[160] The only point I need make here is that it was widely accepted that this Gospel is to be associated with Matthew, but that it is *not* the source of our canonical Greek Matthew.[161]

In returning to Irenaeus and Papias we cannot ask whether the Nazaraean 'Matthew' is to be identified with the Aramaic document to which they refer. We can get nowhere with Irenaeus; there is no evidence that he had even seen the Aramaic document, and, as we have said, his information may itself be derived from Papias. Against this, however, we must note that Irenaeus does not get his information about the place and time of origin for Matthew from anything in our Papias, so either Papias said more which we do not have, or Irenaeus had another source, which for all we know may have been reliable. We can do nothing else but remain agnostic about Irenaeus.

As for Papias himself there is in fact no evidence that he had seen an Aramaic Matthew either. He had heard of an Aramaic Matthew and knew of various Greek versions, one of which he presumably regarded as reasonably authoritative when he wrote his 'Commentary on the Lord's *Logia*'.[162] It would be a natural assumption for Papias to make (Epiphanius made it later) to assume that his Greek Matthew and the (presumably) unseen Aramaic Matthew were basically the same document, and that the Greek was a translation of the Aramaic, but it could well have been a mistaken assumption. In the end we have to remain agnostic about the evidence of Papias also. What can be relied on in his evidence is that there existed an Aramaic text which he thought was the original of Greek Matthew, but whether it really was, or whether it was some other work claiming derivation from Matthew, we simply do not know.

At an earlier stage of our investigation of the thesis that Mark and Matthew depend on a common literary source we eliminated model (B), which may be represented as follows:

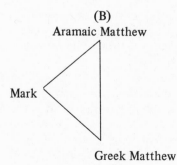

(B)

Aramaic Matthew

Mark

Greek Matthew

It is now time to conclude what we can about model (A), which postulates the direct and unmediated dependence of Mark and Matthew on an Aramaic Matthew. We have to admit that the tradition which attributes

Synoptic material to Matthew is ancient (the superscriptions in the manuscripts may perhaps take us as far back as A.D. 125), but that an Aramaic
Gospel of Matthew depends on the uncertain evidence of Papias alone.
And if there was an Aramaic Gospel Papias would seem to support the
view that the differences between it and canonical Matthew were not great,
so that most of the problems that arise if we posit a dependence of Mark
on canonical Matthew also arise in the case of the hypothetical Matthew.
In other words if we accept the accuracy of Papias' report, we have to
conclude that the postulation of an Aramaic Matthew does not manage to
protect the theory of literary dependence. And we should emphasize yet
again that Papias does not suggest the dependence of Mark on any form of
Matthew, and that his evidence would seem to tell against his having any
such idea.

The time has come to consider our remaining alternative: that Matthew
(neither Aramaic Matthew nor Greek Matthew) is not the source of Mark,
and that Mark is not the source of Matthew. And if we leave such literary
relationships between the Gospels aside, we cannot ignore the possibility
of oral tradition. In examining this alternative I have no wish to suggest
that Mark and Matthew had no written materials at all at their disposal.
Common notes, liturgical fragments, collections of sayings and anecdotes
are still possible, and indeed almost certain, but the major part of the tradition would be oral.

Let us begin by considering the state of the Christian message from A.D.
30 to A.D. 70, a rather brief period of time. The only direct evidence we
have from the Gospels themselves which tells us anything about their formation comes from the opening section of Luke. His words have been
endlessly debated, but certain reasonably firm conclusions can be drawn.
Luke tells us that the events of Jesus' lifetime were handed down
(παρέδοσαν) by the original eyewitnesses and ministers of the word; in
Acts Peter is depicted appealing to his own first-hand experience.[163]
After this 'many people' attempted to produce a narrative version. In
other words there are first of all eyewitness accounts and then written
documents. Luke seems to suggest, though the suggestion may be only
apparent, that it was not the original eyewitnesses that he knew. Be that
as it may, his words confirm what indeed seems likely to have happened.
It seems that most, if not all, of Jesus' earliest followers originally expected that the end of the world would come in their own lifetime. Hence
less pressure to write down accounts of what they knew for future gener-
ations, and a likelihood that, if any of them did write detailed accounts
down, these might well date from, say, twenty years after the events they
recorded. That does not mean, of course, that nothing was in writing

before that time. Above all, letters would have been exchanged between
the early Christian communities. There is no reason to think (and every
reason to deny) that those letters which form part of our New Testament
were the only ones written. And it is possible, certainly, that other written
documents were available in various Christian communities, some of which
may have had a 'liturgical' function, by which must be understood only
that they were regularly read in whole or in part when that community met
together.

After the period of the largely unwritten tradition, we come to Luke's
second stage, the stage at which 'many people put their hand to compiling
a narrative' of the events of Jesus' lifetime. By the time Luke wrote there
were many such attempts, he says. What he does not say is that any one of
these attempts was, in his view, particularly authoritative.[164] From which
it might well follow that similarities between himself and any particular
such source or earlier document might be paralleled *either* in the unwritten
tradition or, in many cases, in other written versions. Luke certainly gives
the impression - some might say disingenuously - of a stage when the
tradition is still the dominant authority, and where the written versions
are to be checked out against the tradition. This account seems eminently
reasonable in view of the attitude of the early believers to which we have
already alluded, and the obvious authority during their lifetimes of the
primary witnesses.

Let us briefly consider the early situation. The original teaching of Jesus
(here I must dogmatize, though I think not dangerously) was largely in
Aramaic, but almost certainly with some admixture of Greek and even
occasionally of Hebrew.[165] Those who first preached his Resurrection
were preaching mainly in Aramaic, though it did not take long before
Greek-speaking Jews became interested. We hear very early of the
'Hellenizers', and soon of conversion among the Gentiles, who were often,
of course, speakers of Greek (or of some other language than Palestinian
Aramaic). Thus the tradition about Jesus must very quickly have come to
exist in at least two languages, Aramaic and Greek. Of course, many of the
original words were in Aramaic, and known to be in Aramaic. Those who
were the primary eyewitnesses knew them, at least originally, in Aramaic.
It is hard to believe that they did not treasure them in as exact a form as
possible - though that is not to suggest, as some have done, that Jesus actually coached them in verbal precision.[166] The point, however, is important.
As the Gospel message spread, it is likely enough that the sayings of Jesus
himself (and to a lesser extent of his disciples) would be preserved with
care, and with a certain concern for verbal accuracy, but that the narrative,
while preserving essentially the same story, would admit of more variations

in detail, and particularly verbally.[167] We may notice in our studies of various passages in Matthew and Mark that this phenomenon often appears; we can now affirm with reasonable certainty that it is highly likely that it would have appeared and that it tells us nothing at all about the certainty or otherwise of literary tradition.

So we have to envisage a large number of stories being told and retold,[168] in two languages, but with the strong likelihood that much care would be lavished on getting things accurate, and above all in recording Jesus' actual words. Nevertheless, as the Christian communities began to grow, some sort of order in the stories would begin to develop. Clearly it was much more important to get the order of events right in some sequences than in others. Above all there would be a very strong pressure to form the Passion-narrative into a continuous and cohesive unit. It might not matter much from the point of view of the early preachers and witnesses whether a particular miracle took place at Cana or at Capernaum; it would be of great significance to make sure that the events after Jesus' arrest and down to his death were told simply, directly and in sequence. Hence the result that Gaboury has so clearly identified: the fixed 'text' of this material seems intelligible at an early date. Intelligible too is the basic set of Synoptic material which I earlier identified as closely parallel in word *and* sequence.

Within the tradition we have briefly outlined, we shall comment on two features. The first is that the 'eyewitnesses' were not all eyewitnesses of every event. In particular, the disciples were not eyewitnesses of the events of Jesus' childhood, though, of course, his family, his mother, and the 'brothers of the Lord', such as James the Just, were. As has often been observed, this fact may be one of the reasons governing Mark's choice of a starting point: he wanted a point where *his* eyewitnesses had first-hand evidence, and perhaps they were only prepared to speak in their own name from the time of Jesus' baptism. In any case it is clear that Jesus' public mission began then, and that the infancy, even the birth of Jesus, played a less prominent part in the lives of ancient Christians than we might have expected from our own experiences of Christianity. But let us leave aside even the matter of the evidence for Jesus' life prior to his baptism. Even when limiting ourselves to events after that time, we have to recognize that not all the 'eyewitnesses and ministers of the word' will provide first-hand evidence. Frequently, the Gospels themselves tell us, for example, Jesus took only a select group, say Peter, James and John. The other disciples must, therefore, have heard of the events on these occasions only from the participants. This point must be duly noted and weighed, without, however, being emphasized in an absurd fashion. It has sometimes been argued, for example, that the Agony in the Garden did not occur because there was no-one there to witness it. Our accounts must, therefore, be (pious?) invention. But Mark's account, when examined without bias must lead us to reject such an interpretation. It is clear that Peter, James and John knew very well what was happening.

Be that as it may, we must admit that we have transmitted versions of the words and deeds of Jesus, of which some had more witnesses, others less. But in general, at least for the events from the appearance of the Baptist to the Ascension, we have an identifiable group of people who are the sources of most of the information, which, for the most part, they had at first hand.[169] And more important, it is not only we who can identify them; they could be identified in first-century Palestine by the communities in which they spoke. This should be emphasized, because it pinpoints a significant issue. In its broad essentials the tradition about Jesus' life is either fact or partial fiction. If it is partial fiction, it is fiction produced, in whatever manner and for whatever reason, largely by the eyewitnesses themselves. Now it must be pointed out that the disadvantages of preaching the new Gospel were many and apparent. Lynching was always a possibility, and expulsion from synagogue a near-certainty. The question has to be asked why such risks should be taken. In other words conscious fraud by the disciples seems unlikely, particularly on matters of primary importance. They knew what had happened to Jesus himself; they had no reason to suppose that a conscious fraud would produce a more immediately satisfactory outcome for themselves.

Although polemicists have enjoyed the conscious-fraud theory from the time of the *De Tribus Impostoribus,* if not before, it has never been widely espoused. More popular have been theories of the gradual accretion of material, whether because of Pauline manipulations (this is the nearest to conscious fraud), liturgical development, or, more insidiously, theological development:[170] the tradition, originally simple and unmiraculous, blossomed into the tales we now possess just as, in the minds of many Two-Documentarians, the simple and primitive Mark expanded into Matthew and Luke. But on this theory, congealed in one of its versions into Krister Stendahl's notion of a 'School of Matthew', we run into the problem of what the eyewitnesses (not to speak of the earliest converts) were doing while the 'history' grew.[171] As we have already observed, it is clear from Paul's letters and above all from Acts that the words and the authority of the eyewitnesses provided the basic evidence on which the Churches were founded. Part of Paul's prestige depended on the fact that he claimed to have 'seen' the Lord in a post-Resurrection appearance, (though there is no evidence that he used this as a device to fabricate elements of Jesus' biography). One of Peter's functions seems to have been to 'confirm' communities established by others; and we cannot but appeal again to Papias who declares in a famous passage that the disciples could provide not book-acquaintance with the Lord but a living and enduring voice.[172]

Let us be clear about the kind of 'development' with which we are concerned. We are not concerned at the moment with what might legitimately be called 'theological development', with, for example, speculations about the Logos such as we find at the beginning of John. We are concerned with the recording of words and deeds which occurred or are alleged to have occurred during Jesus' lifetime. If we assume for the moment that the 'original' teaching of the eyewitnesses was simple, the later complex, laden with theological significance and miraculous, we have to assume that the apostles and the other primary witnesses abetted this development, or that they connived at it, or that it took place against their wishes. But if against their wishes, it is strange that we hear nothing about a struggle between factions in the infant Church, in the way we hear of struggles about the Law, about ritual acts, and above all about circumcision. Indeed at a slightly later date strong reactions to 'Gnostic' developments of Christianity did indeed take place.

In fact for the period before A.D. 70 only three possibilities remain open. Either the tradition from the eyewitnesses was basically unchanged and provided (*in toto*) good evidence for Jesus' words and deeds; *or* the eyewitnesses made fundamental changes from the beginning (such as putting about the Resurrection story when they (or someone) had in fact stolen Jesus' body from the tomb); *or* they were in such a state that they were able to go on believing accounts of Jesus' life which were constantly expanding in the tradition and to forward that expansion by their own testimony or by their own 'theological reflections'. Now we have said that there are good reasons against a 'conscious-fraud' theory; our latter two alternatives therefore boil down to one, namely that the eyewitnesses and ministers of the word were psychologically so affected as to be unable to do more than invent and accept inventions about Jesus' lifetime. As to whether they were in such a state, and why they should have been, is beyond the scope of an essay on the Synoptic Problem.

Whatever we may think about this basic, but nonscholarly problem, one fact remains for us. There is no reason why a mass of stories about Jesus should not have been current, though gradually being reduced to some kind of ordered sequence. It is highly likely that the Passion-narrative would have acquired such a sequence first. Now by A.D. 70 such traditions would certainly have existed in both Greek and Aramaic versions, thus permitting and probably necessitating cross-fertilization between such versions. But there is no reason to assume that the traditions, particularly those deriving from original eyewitnesses, should have been widely divergent. At least the material which deals with the period from Jesus' baptism till his disappearance from the earth should have been retold in constantly overlapping versions. Of course, every time a Christian community met or a preacher preached, the same stories would not have been told - though, as I have said, some, particularly the Passion narrative, would have to be more prominent than others. But some of the same stories would have been told, and in places the sequence of these stories as historical narratives would have been accounted as of little importance. All in all a situation might have existed in the mid-sixties such that our three Synoptics *could* have been written entirely independently of one another. And we should recall that we noted that agreement of words *and order* are not as frequent as might be supposed.

That the Gospel stories did in *fact* circulate in versions similar to, but by no means identical with, the canonical versions seems to be borne out by the patristic evidence. It is not revolutionary to suggest that in the Apostolic Fathers there may be traditions parallel to, rather than derived from, our Gospels.[173] The matter is hard to evaluate because of the small number of texts available (Mark, for example, seems not to be cited before Justin), but the case of Ignatius is particularly enlightening. It is frequently said that Ignatius knew Matthew, but an important recent study has shown how inexact the 'quotations' are and how they often resemble the 'Western' text of Matthew rather than the 'Alexandrian'.[174] In fact it may well be the case that Ignatius does not cite Matthew at all, but merely bears witness to a parallel tradition. We have already noticed Justin's version of the question of the Rich Young Man,[175] and a comparison of sections from the second chapter of Polycarp's letters to the Philippians with the relevant sections of chapters 5 and 7 of Matthew will point in the same direction.

We must, of course, admit, as we have done, that our Synoptic Gospels could *a priori* all be interrelated literary products, but we are now in a position to say that that situation does not command assent as obvious. In fact, since it is an unnecessary hypothesis, the burden of proof lies with its proposers. My theme in the earlier chapters of this book is that in the case of Mark and Matthew many texts which have been alleged to demand a literary theory of derivation demand no such thing. My own view, therefore, is that Matthew and Mark grew up independently on the basis of a similar tradition. I should prefer to think that both of them (and Luke too) came into existence before A.D. 70, though my thesis does not depend on that. Now if my thesis is correct, it does not follow that the texts of Matthew and Mark, as originally composed, were exactly as we now have them. What is demanded is that they were approximately equivalent. It is true that scholars have often been in the habit of 'neutralizing' undesirable sections of these Gospels by shouting 'interpolation' or 'later redaction', and it is likely enough that some changes did indeed take place. But since the names of the 'authors' (Mark, Matthew) were affixed early,[176] and the authority of such versions thus greatly strengthened after the deaths of the original eyewitnesses, we should surely be able to claim that very good arguments for specific interpolations or redactions must be adduced before they can be accepted. Few alleged interpolations are self-evident.

In proposing an oral theory as adequate base for our canonical Gospels of Mark and Matthew, I wish to disassociate myself from two possible versions of that theory, neither of which is necessary and one of which is certainly most unlikely. On the theory of Riesenfeld and Gerhardsson that Jesus actually handed down a verbal tradition to his disciples which they learned by heart from the Master's lips and then passed on to others, the comment of Davies is sufficient: 'Gerhardsson does not deal at length with the question why, if there were a "Holy Word" preserved intact, there was such textual variation'.[177] The more moderate proposal of Gundry,[178] which accounts for the evidence of Papias and for the general dominance of Matthew-like traditions in the patristic evidence on the supposition that Matthew was a more or less official notetaker, cannot be so readily dismissed. Indeed it need not conflict very seriously with my own interpretations, but it must still be received with due scepticism. For if Matthew were any kind of official recorder of events it does seem surprising that our Gospels give no evidence of it. In particular Luke's preface suggests strongly that there was nothing like an official version available when he wrote.

We assume then an oral tradition lying behind the Synoptics, and we have indicated that early patristic evidence seems to indicate that that tradition, as we should expect, did not die the moment the Synoptics were born. Eventually the Synoptics superseded the tradition, and the process probably took longest in those centres like Antioch where the traditions from the eyewitnesses were the oldest and therefore enjoyed the greatest authority. If we hold, as now we must, that the so-called 'Western' readings in our Gospel manuscripts derive from and represent the popular text of the second - century and that the 'P[75] - B' text is an edited version deriving from second century Egypt,[179] we can assume also that the 'Western' readings may include both purely oral variants and variants deriving from the interaction of oral with written tradition. We should further recall that there is no reason to deny that the author of John made further use

of traditional but unwritten material when composing his own Gospel
many years after the Synoptics had appeared.

II

Having briefly returned to the question of the origin of Matthew and to
the mystery of the alleged 'Aramaic Matthew', let us now return to a related issue, but one on which more precision seems to be possible: the
date of Mark. Ancient traditions are clear on the matter. Papias' version
of the origin of Mark, cited by Eusebius, is as follows:[180]
'Mark, having become the "interpreter"of Peter,[181] wrote down accurately
all he recalled, though presenting neither the words nor the acts of the
Lord in sequence. For he had not heard the Lord or followed him, but
later, as I said, he followed Peter. And Peter produced his material in
accordance with the needs of teaching, but not as if compiling a complete
account of the stories about the Lord' (οὐχ ὥσπερ σύνταξιν τῶν
κυριακῶν ποιούμενος λογίων). [182] Clement of Alexandria has a more
elaborate version, which he says is a tradition (παρέδοσαν) of the elders
of a former time:[183] 'When Peter had publicly preached the word in
Rome . . . those present begged Mark . . . to write up what had been said.
When he had done this, he gave the Gospel to those who asked him. When
Peter learned of it later, he neither restrained nor commended.' Finally
there is the evidence of Irenaeus. Irenaeus, we recall, claimed that Matthew
was written while Peter and Paul were preaching - a proposition which is
generally rejected but which I have viewed with more sympathy. Of Mark
he says that 'after the death of Peter and Paul, Mark, the disciple and
"interpreter" of Peter, also handed down in writing the things preached by
Peter.'[184] This version, as is apparent, also makes Mark dependent on
Peter, but allows a somewhat later date, though presumably not too much
later.

   What the tradition says nothing about is any influence of Mark on
Matthew or of Matthew on Mark. It suggests dates for both Gospels between 60 and 70, and suggests Rome as the place of origin for Mark, and
Palestine or Syria for Matthew. Irenaeus, Clement of Alexandria and
Origen, but not Papias, suggest that Matthew was written before Mark, but
indicate no good reasons - Clement offers a rather bad one, namely that
the Gospels with genealogies were composed first - for their belief.[185]
What the ancient traditions do in fact imply is that Matthew and Mark
derive independently from apostolic witness, and this ancient evidence fits
exactly with what I have argued is a most likely interpretation of the evidence of the texts of these Gospels themselves. There is no evidence in

the texts themselves which necessitates literary dependence of Mark on Matthew or of Matthew on Mark; and there is no evidence whatever in the early tradition to indicate that such dependence was thought to have existed.

We have already indicated in Chapter One some of the psychological reasons affecting current orthodoxy on these matters: Mark, the least miraculous of the Gospels, had to be also the most primitive and most authentic. Matthew and Luke, allegedly tied to Markan sequence, displayed many verbal parallels. It was then assumed that regular similarity of sequence demanded literary dependence - which we have found cause to deny. It was assumed that the similarity was so close that it could not be otherwise explained; to which we replied that it was neither as close as was alleged nor was its closeness impossible to explain in other ways. Above all, as Guthrie well summed it up, 'It became almost an axiom of New Testament criticism that at most oral tradition could account for differences, but not similarities.'[186] This axiom, we now suggest, depends on a fundamental misconception of the material available in the years between A.D. 35 and 65. For the 'tradition' in this period is still dependent on the living disciples. Oral tradition among groups that are separate from these disciples depends on their versions of events, and is constantly subject to checking and correction by these eyewitnesses. If one tells the same story, particularly if one is concerned to repeat original words or the gist of original words, as accurately as possible, one is liable indeed to present similarities. It is absurd to suppose that such a tradition could only account for the differences in the Synoptics.

Furthermore, as we have seen, there is no reason to suppose that nothing was in writing, particularly in the larger Churches. There must have been at least letters from the original eyewitnesses, often describing in similar ways the basic events of Jesus' lifetime, in particular the Passion narrative. So as long as we can accept - and we have argued that there is no good reason to deny - that the Synoptics could all have been composed before the end of the first century, and probably by A.D. 70, during the Apostolic Age itself, we find no reason to assert literary dependence as the necessary source of their similarities. In fact, as our detailed analyses have shown, literary dependence is most unlikely between Matthew and Mark. Why then should we not accept the ancient tradition about the independent origin of these works at roughly the same period of time?

The theory that Mark is the source of Matthew is a scholarly thesis with ideological overtones; the theory that Matthew is the source of Mark is older, dating back to Augustine, who supposed Mark to be a mere summary. We have pointed to the serious difficulties of this in a number of

our own examples; and we have to endorse the view of modern criticism
that the crisp and lucid stories are hard to explain as summaries, particularly when they often give more exact and precise detail than their
Matthaean parallels. In fact Augustine's version of literary dependence has
no more to be said for it than the Two-Document alternative. And for all
the skill with which Butler and others defend a version of it, we must not
forget that it too is quite alien to the most ancient patristic evidence.

If we reject the dependence of Mark on Matthew and the dependence
of Matthew on Mark, what becomes of the hypothetical Q? Since I have
not examined (and am not in fact prepared to reject) the likelihood of the
literary dependence of Luke on Mark, the argument for Q might still remain. Thus Q could be one of the sources of Matthew, and together with
Mark, also one of the sources of Luke. But whatever answer we give to
this question depends on what we think Q consisted of in the first place.
Scholars in fact have tended to give up the search for the precise contents
of Q and to use the symbol merely to indicate unidentifiable material, of
which, of course, there is a good deal. But if there ever was a document
to which it would be appropriate to give the title Q, we need not perhaps
be so disturbed at its disappearance now that we can be certain that it can
have had no generally recognized official status whatever. We should recall
that it took many years before our own canonical Gospels attained such
status.

Where do we go from here? We go back to the situation in the early
patristic period when Mark and Matthew were independent documents,
the surviving witnesses of a thirty-year-long and largely oral tradition. And
we may, *if we wish,* accept those writers who make Matthew earlier, but
only provided we do not argue from priority in time (however minimal) to
literary paternity. Perhaps it may be pointed out in addition that the credi-
bility of at least some of the tradition is strengthened by its being represented to us by two rather than by one identifiable primary document.
If that is so, it cannot be helped. 'Christians' and others will simply have
to put up with it.

APPENDIX A

M.D. GOULDER ON THE SYNOPTIC PROBLEM

Recently a most learned student of the Synoptic Problem has been bold enough to push the theory of Markan priority to its logical extreme. In *Midrash and Lection in Matthew* (London 1974) M.D. Goulder proposes that Mark's Gospel is the earliest of the Synoptics, and that Matthew had almost no other evidence about the life of Jesus than Mark. His Gospel, therefore, is a kind of expansion, or revised second edition, of Mark. Luke, when his time came, wrote a Gospel based on Mark and Matthew together, with Mark as his primary source. Matthew's Gospel, according to Goulder, is thus related to Mark in a somewhat similar way to that in which Chronicles is related to Kings. This attractively radical proposal certainly removes many of the obstacles which have impeded Markan priority in the past: Mark is now indisputably the only source for the researcher who would like to write a biography of Jesus, and almost all Matthaean and Lucan variants can be summarily dismissed as pious fictions. But although removing certain traditional difficulties Goulder's thesis introduces others of so serious a nature that it must apparently be rejected almost in its totality. What will remain as of permanent value are Goulder's perceptive and detailed identifications of the basic characteristics of Matthew's Gospel as we have it.

The following objections to Goulder's proposal seem in many cases individually, and certainly cumulatively, decisive against it:

(1) The phenomena of time and context preclude any serious comparison between Kings/Chronicles and Mark/Matthew.

(2) Goulder has to assume that the purpose of all the Synoptic Gospels is liturgical. They are not primarily, or even substantially, intended as historical records of Jesus. Mark can be divided as lections for the year from New Year to Easter; Matthew is suited to the whole Jewish-Christian year. Now although it is doubtless possible that the two Gospels could have been so divided - but why did Mark only write

for part of the year? - there is no evidence whatever that they were actually so treated in early Christian times.

(3)   Goulder's view that before the appearance of Mark virtually no 'non-Markan' traditions about the life of Jesus were available even in Palestine seems fantastic. Thousands of people must have heard Jesus, and at least hundreds more talked to the primary witnesses at Jerusalem. Goulder (pp. 140 - 1) tries to minimize this by assuming not only that very quickly the tradition became monolithic, centred on Peter, James and John, and only defectively available outside Jerusalem - which might possibly be true - but that there were almost no authentic stories about Jesus available outside Jerusalem, or even outside a tiny group inside - which is unlikely. Furthermore he has to assume that Mark's Gospel virtually exhausts the material even available to Peter, James and John - which is incredible. In order to buttress his claim, Goulder is driven to assume that on the view of those who insist on the existence of 'non - Markan' traditions, Matthew's Church must have thrown away much traditional evidence when Mark arrived (p. 147).

(4)   Goulder's assumption that on the appearance of Mark all sorts of Churches began to write Gospels for their own purposes lends Mark an authority for which there is no ancient evidence, and which is implicitly denied by Luke (1:1). Luke mentions no peculiarly authoritative source, neither Mark nor anyone else.

(5)   Goulder's theory that Matthew is midrash on Mark, and Luke on both of them, entails, as he admits, that Matthew and Luke simply invented whole incidents which they claimed as history. We are dealing in the Infancy Narrative, for example, not merely with the re-writing or editing of a tradition, but with its inception. Furthermore, even if we might credit Matthew, the Jewish-Christian 'scribe' writing for Jews, with such activity, it is much harder to suppose that Luke has done the same thing. And if he has not, then there were traditions other than those represented by Mark.

(6)   A strict employment (or *reductio*) of Goulder's principle might dispense with Mark as a historical source also. Matthew's inventiveness in non-Markan passages need hardly allow itself to be circumscribed so much in Markan passages. In other words on the midrash theory it is precisely those features of Matthew which are very close to Mark which are the hardest to explain. Goulder seems aware of this difficulty when he suggests (for example on p. 35) that the phenomenon of fatigue on Matthew's part is

adequate to illustrate why after chapter 13 Matthew follows Mark's order 'with hardly a variation', whereas in chapters 1 - 12 he 'rearranges Mark freely'. But this explanation is peculiarly flimsy in view of the fact that according to Goulder himself the midrash (i.e. Matthew) took from five to ten years to compose. Goulder, of course, needs the latter argument to help exorcize the spectre of Stendahl's 'rabbinic School of Matthew'.

(7) Goulder starts (p. 4) with the assumption that Matthew had Mark in front of him, and then shows how Matthew has altered and 'overwritten' Mark. He thus never seriously investigates alternative possibilities and, on the axiom of no non-Markan traditions, has no difficulty in indicating that Matthew *could* be over-written Mark. Goulder's process of thought might be re-constructed thus: Any document that looks something like Mark but is larger than Mark depends on Mark; Matthew is such a document; therefore Matthew depends on Mark.

(8) On pp. 474 - 5 Goulder produces a statistical 'proof' that Matthew is not overwriting Q or M in non-Markan passages. He claims (i) that in Markan passages 18% of Matthew's words are characteristically Matthaean; (ii) that of *non-Markan* passages 28½% are characteristically Matthaean. He then argues that if the midrash theory is right, characteristically Matthaean words should form approximately 28½% of the total Q and M passages - which they more or less do. But if there are 'alien sources' in Q and M passages, the percentage of characteristic words should be about 18% - which it is not. But even granting Goulder's data, we should not concede that he has proved that there are no alien sources. A Two-Documentarian could observe that the 'proof' merely shows that Matthew had more respect for Mark than for Q or M. Thus even on the assumption of Markan priority it does not follow that no other sources were available.

Our conclusion can only be that Goulder's approach to the Synoptic problem must be rejected. On Goulder's principles any text bearing some relation to the narrative of Mark can be 'explained' as midrash on Mark.

NOTES

1   W. R. Farmer, *The Synoptic Problem* (New York 1964).

2   B. H. Streeter, *The Four Gospels* (London 1924).

3   E.g. by H. G. Jameson, *The Origin of the Synoptic Gospels* (Oxford 1922); J. Chapman, *Matthew, Mark and Luke. A Study in the Order and Interrelations of the Synoptic Gospels* (Privately printed 1937); B. C. Butler, *The Originality of St Matthew* (Cambridge 1951). Note Butler's demonstration that many of the arguments used by Streeter and others to demonstrate Markan priority can in fact only be used to show the priority of an hypothetical Ur-Markus, the existence of which is now, and for good reasons, generally denied.

4   'The Priority of Mark' in *The Birth of the New Testament,* 2nd edn. (ed. C. F. D. Moule, London 1966) 232, n. 2.

5   Note the comment of X. Léon-Dufour on the contemporary consensus in 'Redaktionsgeschichte of Matthew and Literary Criticism', in *Jesus and Man's Hope I* (Pittsburgh 1970) 9: 'To be orthodox in the exercise of Redaktionsgeschichte "in the strict sense", one has to admit the system of literary criticism called the Two-Source Theory'.

6   See, for example, much of the material in *L'Evangile selon Matthieu* (ed. M. Didier, Gembloux 1972), especially the papers of M. Devisch and F. Neirynck.

7   Cf. Aug., *de cons. ev.* 1. 2. 4.

8   B. C. Butler, *The Originality of St Matthew,* 166 - 8.

9   L. Vaganay, *Le Problème Synoptique: une hypothèse de travail* (Tournai-Paris 1954).

10 J. J. Griesbach, *Commentatio qua Marci Evangelium totum e Mattaei et Lucae Commentariis Decerptum esse monstratur* (Jena 1789 - 90). Much criticism of the Griesbach theory has been merely emotional, but there are substantial objections

to it. Above all the argument we discuss below in connection
with the possible dependence of Mark on Matthew alone becomes
doubly relevant. If a community had both Matthew and Luke,
who would want Mark? Farmer thinks that Mark's Gospel was
composed (perhaps at Alexandria or Rome) to satisfy Christians
from different parts of the world who were used to different
Gospels, some to Matthew, some to Luke, etc. It was thus something for everybody, consisting mainly of favourite passages bearing
'concurrent testimony to the same Gospel tradition' (W. R. Farmer,
The Synoptic Problem, 280). But, as Fitzmyer points out, why has
Mark not used some at least of the Double Tradition? Is our Double
Tradition *all* material of secondary importance? Farmer seems to
imply that we explain these omissions simply because the passages
are not in the same order and sequence in Matthew and Luke - hence
the omission of the Lord's Prayer! For further comments see J. A.
Fitzmyer, 'The Priority of Mark and the "Q" Source in Luke', in
Jesus and Man's Hope (Pittsburgh 1970) especially 135, 160 - 2.
At n. 99 Fitzmyer lists various reviews of Farmer. See also A.
Gaboury, *La Structure des Evangiles synoptiques* (Leiden 1970) 27.

11   D. L. Dungan, 'Mark - The Abridgement of Matthew and Luke', in
Jesus and Man's Hope I (Pittsburgh 1970) 55.

12   For a more detailed (and up-to-date) outline of the arguments of
the Markan priorists, see J. A. Fitzmyer, in *Jesus and Man's Hope I,*
134 - 47.

13   An exception is the Cleansing of the Temple at Mt 21:12 - 13 =
Lk 19:45 - 6; cf. Mk 11:15 - 17.

14   There is no need to say more about Streeter's 'fifth point' in favour
of Markan priority, namely that verbal agreements between Matthew
and Luke against Mark can easily be explained away. Streeter used
different techniques to 'explain away' the inconvenient evidence,
a method dubbed 'atomization of the phenomena' by Farmer (*The
Synoptic Problem,* 118; cf. Dungan, in *Jesus and Man's Hope I,*
57ff.). The effect of the method is to neglect the cumulative im-
pact of the agreements. Individually they can then be dismissed
as either insignificantly trivial coincidences, or due to textual corruption, or the overlap of Mark and Q. Most thus disappear, and
the few 'hard cases' can be the more easily disposed of. See
Farmer, Butler and A. M. Farrer, 'On Dispensing with Q', *Studies
in the Gospels: Essays in Memory of R. H. Lightfoot* (ed. D. E.
Nineham, Oxford 1957) 55 - 88.

15   The problem would not be affected if we accepted Stendahl's

'rabbinic' School of Matthew, for we should then be concerned
with some member or members of the school deploying his text of
Mark (See K. Stendahl, *The School of St Matthew* (Uppsala 1954).)

16   See note 10 above. It could not be argued that Matthew is 'too
Jewish' for a Roman audience; that does not account for the
omissions. The *Diatessaron* does not provide a parallel to Mark's
supposed procedure, for it does contain such items as the Nativity
which Mark excludes. Streeter's word on this topic is still authoritative: 'Only a lunatic would leave out Matthew's account of the
Infancy, the Sermon on the Mount and practically all the parables,
in order to get room for purely verbal expansion of what remains'
(my italics; Streeter, *The Four Gospels,* 158).

17   Dungan, *op. cit.* 93 - 4, with Irenaeus, *Adv. Haer.* 1.27.2; Epiph.,
Pan. 42.11.

18   If the author of 'Matthew' was in fact the apostle Matthew, there
is no reason to accept the oft-quoted view that he would not have
relied on a text provided by the non-apostolic Mark. Matthew might
even have been humble enough to recognize in Mark a fellow eyewitness and an honest man, even though not one of the Twelve. But
no comment on the relationship between 'Matthew' and Matthew
would be appropriate at this point.

19   I leave aside for the moment the extreme but implausible view that
Matthew had virtually no material about Jesus' life other than the
text of Mark.

20   E.g. by M. D. Goulder, *Midrash and Lection in Matthew* (London
1974) 280.

21   No credence can be put in the claim of J. O'Callaghan that fragments
of Mark dating from about A.D. 50 have turned up in Cave 7 at
Qumran ('¿Papiros neotestamentarios en la cueva 7 de Qumran?'),
Biblica 53 (1972) 91 - 100. Contra, J. Vardaman, 'The Earliest
Fragments of the New Testament', *ET* 83 (1972) 374 - 6; and K.
Aland, 'Neue Neutestamentliche Papyri III', *NTS* 20 (1974) 357 - 81.

22   On Proto-Luke see especially Streeter, *The Four Gospels* 199 - 222;
and V. Taylor, *The Formation of the Gospel Tradition* (London
1933), Appendix A, 191 - 201. The Proto-Luke theory has the advantage of allowing a sequence: Proto-Luke, Acts, Luke, thus giving
a later date for Acts and hence for Luke.

23   *Adv. Haer.* 3.1.2 (Eus., *Historia Ecclesiastica (H.E.)* 5.8.3).

24   *Ap.* Eus., *H.E.* 6.14.6. This may derive from Papias (*ap.* Eus.,
3.39.15), though there is the additional 'information' that Peter
neither approved nor disapproved. If Morton Smith's supposed

letter of Clement *(Clement of Alexandria and a Secret Gospel of Mark*
(Harvard 1973)) is genuine, there is evidence that 'Clement' thought
that an *original* version of Mark appeared in Peter's lifetime (fol. one,
ll .15 - 16), though again I am inclined to suspect that Papias is the
source of 'Clement's' information (cf. with Papias at *H.E.* 3.39.15)
about the nature of Mark's relationship to Peter. And there still remains the possibility that Smith's 'Clement' got his information from
the *H.E.* of Eusebius itself.

25   Cf. *par excellence* G. D. Kilpatrick, *The Origins of the Gospel according to St Matthew* (Oxford 1946), especially 110ff., 140. Kilpatrick
offers a date for Matthew between A.D. 90 and 100.

26   Kilpatrick's attempt to associate Matthew with scribal activity after
A.D. 70 fails. As N. B. Stonehouse explains *(Origins of the Synoptic
Gospels* (Grand Rapids, Mich. 1965) 29), Kilpatrick makes much too
extreme a distinction between the 'earlier Judaism' and the 'Rabbinical
Judaism' of the Talmud which he finds reflected in Matthew. In general Kilpatrick seems to equate 're-Judaizing' in Matthew with whole-
sale rewriting - which is not transparent.

27   Mt 5:11, 23:34, 10:7, etc. 'suggest more violent local outbursts than
the sobriety of Jamnia' (W. D. Davies, *The Setting of the Sermon on
the Mount* (Cambridge 1964) 297).

28   Josephus, *Antiquities of the Jews* 20.9.1.

29   Observe the comments of D. R. Catchpole, *The Trial of Jesus* (Leiden
1971) 127.

30   Irenaeus, *Adv. Haer.* 3.1.2.

31   Streeter, *The Four Gospels,* 291, and (e.g.) C. H. Dodd, *The Parables
of the Kingdom* (London 1941) 189ff.

32   A good example of this can be seen if we compare Mt 24:45 with
Lk 12:41 - 2. The ἄρα in the text is appropriate in Luke, inapprop-
riate in Matthew as it stands. Cf. C.F.D. Moule, in *The Birth of the
New Testament* 147 - 8.

33   C. F. Burney, *The Poetry of Our Lord* (Oxford 1925) 87 - 8.

34   *Ap. H.E.* 3.39.20.

35   For a summary of the discussion see R. McL. Wilson, *Studies in the
Gospel of Thomas* (London 1960) 146.

36   But not a fifth Gospel; cf. A. F. J. Klijn, *A Survey of the Researches
into the Western Text of the Gospels and Acts, Part II*, 1949 - 1969
(Leiden 1969) 8 - 26.

37   B. C. Butler, *The Originality of St Matthew.*

38   A. Farrer, in *Studies in the Gospels.*

39   See J. A. Fitzmyer, in *Jesus and Man's Hope I.* The recent attempt

by Goulder (*Midrash and Lection in Matthew*, 452 - 73) to show Luke's dependence on Matthew is open to similar objections to those that may be brought against his treatment of Matthew itself. See Appendix pp. 109—11.

40   'St Mark's Knowledge and Use of Q', in *Oxford Studies in the Synoptic Problem* (ed. W. Sanday, Oxford 1911) 169 - 71. Cf. E. P. Sanders, 'The Overlaps of Mark and Q and the Synoptic Problem', *NTS* 19 (1973) 453 - 65.

41   *The Four Gospels,* 211; cf. B. C. Butler, *The Originality of St Matthew,* 8 - 13.

42   For a selection of versions of the content of Q, see T. W. Manson, *The Sayings of Jesus* (London 1964) 16.

43   *Op. cit.,* 225.

44   K. Stendahl (*The School of St Matthew,* 32 - 3) claims implausibly that 'ministers of the word' refers to a type of minor synagogue official or keeper of documents.

45   For comments on authenticity, primitivity, etc., see following text. On 'poor in spirit' see Farrer, in *Studies in the Gospels,* 64. For the view that the addition of 'in spirit' may not change the sense but merely make it explicit see R. H. Gundry, *The Use of the Old Testament in St Matthew's Gospel with special reference to the Messianic Hope* (*Nov. Test.* Supp. 18, Leiden 1967) 70.

46   There are almost no agreements *of order* between Matthew and Luke against Mark. So, recently, H. G. Wood, review of Butler, *E.T.* 1953, 17ff. Of course if Luke *knew* that Mark was prior to Matthew, he would follow him more slavishly. But if he had such knowledge, we have a more weighty problem on our hands with the sections where Luke abandons Mark's account for some other. Above all why should he do that if he knew that Mark *alone* reflects authentic Christian tradition, as supposed by Goulder, *Midrash and Lection in Matthew,* 452 - 73?

47   Perhaps it should also be noted in passing here that it seems most unlikely that Luke knows Matthew's version of the Sermon on the Mount.

48   See especially Butler, *The Originality of St Matthew,* 24 - 61.

49   Cf. Jn 9:1 - 7.

50   Cf. E. P. Sanders, *The Tendencies of the Synoptic Tradition* (SNTS Monograph Series No.9, Cambridge 1969). Note especially the summary on 275.

51   In the course of this study I shall allude to three out of five of Streeter's main arguments for the priority of Mark, and reject them.

These are the arguments (1) from shared material, (2) from the order
of sections and parts of sections, and (3) from 'primitivity'. It should
appear *en passant* why these arguments are inconclusive. For a re-
buttal of (2), see E. P. Sanders, 'The Argument from Order and the
Relationship between Matthew and Luke', *NTS* 15(1969)249 - 61.
Streeter has two further approaches which have already been ade-
quately rebutted. For his treatment of 'minor agreements' between
Matthew and Luke against Mark, see note 14, and observe also that
Streeter virtually ignored agreements of Matthew and Luke about
omissions from the Markan narrative.

    Streeter also claimed that 'subsequent to the Temptation story,
there is not a single case in which Matthew and Luke agree in inserting a piece of Q material . . . into the same context of Mark'. This
was rejected by H. G. Jameson (*The Origin of the Synoptic Gospels,*
15ff.) who commented that Streeter himself frequently noted that
'Luke does not attempt to insert his "Q" matter into the Markan
context at all, but collects it all into some three or four large sections'.
Butler (*The Originality of St Matthew,* 67) added that this 'argument'
of Streeter's *depends* on the Two-Document theory and is not therefore a proof of the validity of that theory.

52   Gaboury, *La Structure des Evangiles Synoptiques.* I am not, however, prepared to follow Gaboury in his view (221ff.) that Luke knew
the Passion narrative (Gaboury's section C (ommun)) at an earlier
stage of its formation than Mark and Matthew, nor that Matthew
knew the teaching material (section D(ifferent)) at an earlier stage
than Mark and Luke. These distinctions, as will appear, are too ab-
solute and depend on the notion of a single pre-canonical source
used in a rather similar fashion by the three Evangelists. Nor do I
follow Gaboury's further subdivision of section D. Nevertheless the
book is important and cannot be neglected. Naturally it has aroused
comment; the most interesting is perhaps that of F. Neirynck, 'A
Critical Analysis of A. Gaboury's Hypothesis', in *L'Evangile selon
Matthieu* (ed. M. Didier, Gembloux 1972) 37 - 69. Neirynck is
effective as a critic of the subdivision of D.

53   W. R. Farmer, *Synopticon* (Cambridge 1969).

54   A. Gaboury, *L'Evangile selon Matthieu,* 221.

55   After the theological preface John's Gospel also begins with John
the Baptist, and the same passage of Isaiah (40:3) is quoted. Cf.
Peter's preaching at Acts 11:37.

56   We may note here the Aramaic (?) βασιλεία τῶν οὐρανῶν absent
from Mark and Luke. For parallels see Butler, *The Originality of*

St Matthew, 148. Butler indicates that the phrase occurs thirty-two times in Matthew.

57 Unless the explanation, as some have held, is that Matthew, intending to emphasize that forgiveness of sins is the prerogative of Jesus, deliberately omits it here to heighten the contrast between Jesus and John. Mt 3:13ff. would support an interpretation of this sort.

58 'St Mark's Knowledge and use of Q', in *Oxford Studies in the Synoptic Problem* (ed. W. Sanday, Oxford 1911), 168. For the following discussion see especially Sanders, 'The Overlaps of Mark and Q and the Synoptic Problem', *NTS* 19 (1973) 459.

59 Cf. note 57 above. Matthew may have a 'Palestinian' concern to affirm the superiority of Jesus to John (against some of John's latter-day followers?).

60 Jerome (*Adv. Pel.* 3.2) knows of versions of Mt 3:13ff. as given in the Gospel according to the Hebrews, an expansion of Matthew and therefore, perhaps, evidence that Matthew originally contained *some* material of this kind.

61 D, it., Justin, Clement, etc.

62 Sanders, 'The Overlaps of Mark and Q', especially 461, 464.

63 Sanders, 'The Overlaps of Mark and Q' 464; cf. also his 'Priorités et dépendances dans la tradition synoptique', *Rech. Sci. Rel.* 60 (1972) 519 - 40, esp. 539, 'La solution la plus probable du problème synoptique pourrait faire appel à un Evangile Primitif (Ur-Gospel) ou *mieux encore* [my italics] maintenir qu'un ou plusieurs évangiles ont été édités après avoir été utilisés par l'autre (ou par les autres)'.

64 So Streeter, 'St Mark's Knowledge', 168.

65 Cf. Butler, *The Originality of St Matthew,* 112 - 13.

66 Streeter, *op. cit.* 168.

67 At 4:4 Luke omits 'but by every word that proceeds from the mouth of God'.

68 Luke has already referred to the arrest at 3:19 - 20 and does not repeat himself.

69 Mark is fond of the phrase 'the Gospel' (1:15, 10:29, 13:10, 14:9); cf. Butler, *The Originality of St Matthew* 118 - 19.

70 Luke causes unnecessary confusion by relating the story of Simon's mother-in-law, and thus introducing Simon (4:38) before the call of Simon itself (5:1 - 11). This obscure presentation of events seems to be the result of Luke's wishing to follow the Markan order of events at Capernaum.

71 See Butler, *The Originality of St Matthew,* 124 - 5.

72 Gerasa seems to be the oldest reading we can obtain from the MSS,

though it cannot be the original text of Mark, since Gerasa is too far from the sea of Galilee. Mark presumably wrote Gergesa, and this remote name was soon replaced by something better known in the copy (or copies) of Mark's text.

73 Sanders, 'Priorités et dépendances dans la tradition synoptique', 535 - 6.

74 G. D. Kilpatrick, *The Origins of the Gospel of St Matthew*, 110 - 11.

75 'Their' synagogues also occurs in Mt 9:35, 12:9, 13:54 and - important evidence against supposing that 'their' synagogues is post-Jamnian - in Mk 1:23 and 39, which are all sections of narrative. It does not occur in the words of Jesus at Mt 6:2 and 5, or 23:6. At Mt 10:17, however, Jesus' words do include 'their'.

76 This striking word is replaced by something tamer in Luke ($\pi\alpha\rho\dot{\eta}\gamma\gamma\epsilon\iota\lambda\epsilon\nu$; 5:14).

77 The hand of a redactor has been 'detected' as in part accounting for this. J. Weiss, for example, thought that the reference to 'carried by four men' could be so explained (*Das älteste Evangelium* (Göttingen 1903) 155).

78 Also 'his', viz. Levi's, house (omitted in Matthew).

79 So M. D. Goulder, *Midrash and Lection in Matthew*, 325.

80 Some would say the attitude of the primitive community. For an example of how this 'conclusion' may be reached, see T. A. Burkill, *New Light on the Earliest Gospel* (Ithaca 1972) 39.

81 Matthew also omits the 'leaven of Herod' of Mk 8:15, replacing it with a reference to Sadducees. Some might suppose this argues a later date (or redaction) for Matthew. But such arguments need to be treated with care. Matthew has as many references to Sadducees (seven) as the rest of the New Testament together. How so if Matthew is, let us say, after Jamnia? If such a date explains omissions of Herodians,, it would not explain emphasis on Sadducees. Kilpatrick's attempt to equate Sadducees with non-Pharisaic Jews is bizarre (*The Origins of the Gospel of St Matthew*, 121).

82 Sanders ('The Overlaps of Mark and Q and the Synoptic Problem', 460) argues that Matthew is either a conflation of Mark and Q or a source of Mark and Luke, and that it is a middle term between Mark and Luke.

Goulder (*Midrash and Lection in Matthew* 40 - 1) argues that the improper suggestion that the Lord had been out of his mind (Mk 3:20) is excised by transferring the verb $\dot{\epsilon}\xi\iota\sigma\tau\dot{\alpha}\nu\alpha\iota$ to the crowds (Mt 12:23). This is supposed to explain what is in fact the *absence* from Matthew of a whole incident in Mark. For the problem of

Matthew's alleged bowdlerizing see Chapter Four.

83 The technique has been dubbed 'The Law of the Drunkard's Search'
    by A. Kaplan, in *The Conduct of Inquiry: Methodology for
    Behavioural Science* (San Francisco 1964) 11, 17, 18. Cf. T. F.
    Carney, *Phoenix* 27 (1973) 168. An example: if you walk down a
    dark street and lose your wallet, make sure you only look for it under
    the single street light, because the light is better there.

84 Some, of course, think that this 'body of material' is Matthew. Butler
    (*The Originality of St Matthew,* 93) sees the whole of Mk 4:1 - 34 as
    an excerpt, but his arguments are not conclusive.

85 Note the reference to fringes and phylacteries at Mt 23:5.

86 Cf. R. McL. Wilson, *Studies in the Gospel of Thomas* (London 1960)
    98; and in general G. Garitte, 'Les Parables du Royaume dans
    l'évangile de Thomas', *Le Muséon* 70 (1957) 307 - 10, and L. Cerfaux,
    ibid., 311 - 27.

87 I should like to thank J. W. Wevers for checking the Coptic.

88 παρά + Acc. = 'along' in all Synoptics. J. Wellhausen (*Das Evangelium
    Marci* (Berlin 1903)) thought it should be 'on' the road, not 'beside'
    the road. C. C. Torrey (*Our Translated Gospels* (New York 1936) 7)
    claimed that Aramaic 'al 'urha is ambiguous.

89 The substitution of 'no root' for 'no moisture' at Lk 8:13 suggests
    that the reading ἰκμάδα may be corrupt.

90 R. H. Gundry (*The Use of the Old Testament in St Matthew's Gospel
    with special reference to the Messianic Hope* (*Nov. Test.* Supp. 18,
    Leiden 1967) 33 - 4) and others seem not to find Matthew 'gentler'
    or 'softer'. That is hard to accept, whatever the explanation.

91 Cf. (for example) Styler, 'The Priority of Mark' in *The Birth of the
    New Testament,* 2nd edn. (ed. C. F. D. Moule, London 1966) 228.

92 Cf. M. Black, *An Aramaic Approach to the Gospels and Acts,* 3rd
    edn. (Oxford 1957) 212ff. For many other problems of the d^e
    particle, *ibid.* 76 - 83. On 215 Black comments, 'Matthew's depend-
    ence on a source other than Mark is evidence that the quotation oc-
    curred in a genuine saying of Jesus'.

93 Nevertheless Butler's argument that Mk 13:33 - 7 is a telescoped
    version of Mt 24:37 - 25:46 does not convince me. Dependence on
    Matthew is certainly not necessary.

94 Butler, *The Originality of St Matthew,* 135.

95 Similar comment could be made about the ἔχειν τι occurring in
    Mt 5:23 and Mk 11:25.

96 All of which we have discussed or will discuss.

97 Streeter, 'St Mark's Knowledge and Use of Q', in *Oxford Studies in*

the Synoptic Problem (ed. W. Sanday, Oxford 1911) 173. Cf.
Sanders, 'The Overlaps of Mark and Q and the Synoptic Problem',
456.

98   On the whole problem see especially Sanders' summary of the evidence (*The Tendencies of the Synoptic Tradition,* (Cambridge 1969)
275).

99   Sanders, 'Priorités et dépendances dans la tradition synoptique',
520 - 30, especially 525.

100 Butler, *The Originality of St Matthew,* 134; cf. Sanders, *op. cit.,*
529 - 30.

101 Justin (*Dial.* 101) preserves a 'mixed version' of this story, perhaps
derived from none of our written Gospels: his text reads 'Why do
you call me good? One is good, my father in the heavens'.

102 See p.44.

103 Streeter (*The Four Gospels,* 159) holds that Luke deliberately sub-
stitutes a non-Markan source (L) for a Markan in this passage. Cf.
similar remarks on the call of Peter, the Anointing and the Passion
narrative generally. Butler (*The Originality of St Matthew,* 129)
agrees that Lk 4:22 is not dependent on Mark.

104 P⁴⁵ and others assimilate Mark to Matthew at this point, and Origen
(*C. Cels.* 6.34, 36) claims that none of the Gospels refers to Jesus as
himself a carpenter. Butler (*The Originality of St Matthew,* 129)
claims that Mark changes Matthew because he has not given an account of Jesus' birth!! But we may ask (from the point of view of
the people of Nazareth): What is the difference between describing
Jesus as a carpenter or as the son of a carpenter?

105 E.g. recently by Styler, 'The Priority of Mark' in *The Birth of the
New Testament,* 2nd edn. (ed. C. F. D. Moule, London 1966) 228.

106 At 14:9 Matthew has 'king'. M. D. Goulder (*Midrash and Lection
in Matthew,* 35) puts this down to 'fatigue', and 'The magnet of the
text he is following'. This would be more plausible if the rest of
Matthew's account were slavishly close to Mark! Goulder even in-
vokes a similar principle to 'explain' why he thinks that in chapters
1 - 12 Matthew 'rearranges Mark freely', while after chapter 13 'he
follows Mark's order with hardly a variation'. It seems hardly necessary to argue that this is a desperate proposal.

If we follow D (and others) for the text of Matthew and omit the
name Philip, Matthew is precise (whether by luck or by judgment)
in another regard. For Herodias was not originally the wife of Herod
Philip, but the wife of Herod, son of Mariamne. In any case, of course,
Herodias' first husband was not Antipas' brother, but his half-brother.

Since the version of D etc., is historically correct, we must probably
either assume that it represents a better version of the original text
of Matthew, or (much less likely) a correction of an earlier text of
Matthew by someone well-acquainted with the historical facts. If
D is original Matthew here, it is evidence against Matthew following
Mark. In general see Josephus, *Ant.* 18. 5. 4 and E. Schurer (revised),
The History of the Jewish People in the age of Jesus Christ (London
1973) 344, n.19.

107   Streeter thought of an overlap of Mark and M. R. Bultmann, implausibly as we shall argue, held that Matthew has corrected the text
of Mark on the basis of a like tradition (*Die Geschichte* 277, n.1).
The suggestion (recently made again by Burkill, *New Light on the
Earliest Gospel,* 76) that Matthew only indicates that Jesus went 'in
the direction of Tyre and Sidon' may be dismissed.

108   Butler (*The Originality of St Matthew,* 131) claims that it is incon-
ceivable that a late 'Matthew' re-Judaized this passage: 'No one,
addressing himself to a Gentile Christian Church after about A.D.50,
could fail to feel difficulties in Matthew's account.' But this seems
to beg too many questions.

109   For an explanation of Magadan and Dalmanutha as derived from
Migdal Nuna or Nunaiya see J. Finegan, *The Archaeology of the
New Testament* (Princeton 1969) 46.

110   Note that at Mt 14:33 (not paralleled in Mark, who has 'their hearts
were hardened') the disciples worship Jesus as 'the son of God'. This
precedes the 'confession' at Caesarea Philippi and is possibly mis-
placed. More likely, however, Mark represents the original version
and Matthew's text has been 'doctored' at some stage in the tradition.

111   The attempt of O. Cullmann to shift Mt 16:17 - 19 to a confession
of Peter in the Upper Room (Peter: *Disciple, Apostle and Martyr,*
2nd edn. (trans. F. V. Filson, Philadelphia 1962) 61 - 3, 176 - 91))
is refuted by R. H. Gundry, 'The Narrative Framework of Mt 16:17 -
19', *Nov. Test.* 7 (1964) 1 - 9.

112   E.g., K. Kundsin, *Primitive Christianity in the Light of Gospel
Research* (Harper Torchbook edition, New York, 1962) 144 - 7.

113   For ἐκκλησία see Deut. 31:30 etc. To say that Jesus may have
envisaged an organization is not to imply that he intended to separate
his movement from Judaism. Rather the 'Church' could act as a
'cell' which was intended eventually to swallow Judaism as a whole.
More generally see W. H. Brownlee, 'Messianic Motifs of Qumran and
the New Testament', *NTS* 3 (1956) 16 - 17. He observes that the
Qumranic Teacher of Righteousness refers to the Qumran community as 'my Council'.

114   According to V. Taylor, *The Gospel according to St Mark* (London
       1952) 379, Matthew's οὐ μὴ ἔσται σοι τοῦτο, supported by Markan
       sources a, b, sy^S for 8:32, is the original text of Mark. Far more
       plausible, however, is the view that the addition in Mark is due to the
       influence of Matthew.

115   For what it is worth, we should perhaps add that this section contains
       two miracles of healing in Mark (with spitting) which have no parallel
       in Matthew or Luke (7:32 - 6, 8:22 - 6). If Matthew knew this ma-
       terial, he has bowdlerized his source, some would say.

116   This is the view of Butler, *The Originality of Matthew*, 139. In gen-
       eral Butler is too inclined to explain doublets as cross-references - an
       unnecessary move if they do not need to be explained away. Farmer,
       The Synoptic Problem, 256, tells us that Mt 5:32 is 'secondary', and
       uses it as evidence that Mark, who knows both the primary and the
       'secondary' Matthew, is at the end of the Synoptic tradition.

117   See note 116.

118   H. Crouzel, 'Le Texte Patristique de Mt V.32 et XIX. 9', *NTS* 19
       (1972 - 3) 98 - 119.

119   I owe this suggestion to Anna T. Rist.

120   Following Harnack, some have seen 'Markan influence'.

121   Did Luke know that the 'divorcée' did not have to remarry in the
       Christian community? Cf. I Cor. 7:10 on 'separated' women.

122   *The Synoptic Problem*, 254.

123   Clem. Rom. I, 46.

124   Matthew's 'in your kingdom' (20:21) may be 'earlier' than Mark's
       'in your glory' (10:37); cf. V. Taylor, *St Mark* (London 1959) 440.

125   Such, of course, has to be the view of Goulder, *Midrash and Lection
       in Matthew*, 35, who thinks that Matthew is out to save the credit
       of James and John. Bowdlerizers neglect the passages in Matthew
       himself where the 'credit' of prominent disciples is lost (e.g. 16:23).
          The mother appears to be Salome (alluded to again, though not
       named, at Mt 27:55 and named by Mk 15:40 and 16:1). Was her
       name suppressed because of the role she played in 'Gnostic' versions
       of Jesus' life?

126   *The Originality of St Matthew*, 135.

127   We should notice that the 'Secret Gospel of Mark' has a version of
       the Lazarus story, occurring at Bethany, after Mk 10:46. There is
       no trace of these additions in Matthew or Luke. And there seems
       something odd about the Lazarus story occurring at Bethany after
       10:34, because at this stage of the narrative Jesus has not yet reached
       Jericho, let alone Bethany, which is nearer Jerusalem.

128   Gundry (*The Use of the Old Testament in St Matthew's Gospel with
      special reference to the Messianic Hope,* 198 - 9) has an interesting
      discussion of the matter of the ass plus young jackass, but fails to
      clarify the question of riding two animals.

129   According to Gundry (*ibid.* 130) Matthew follows the Hebrew text
      very closely here.

130   So P. Winter, *The Trial of Jesus* (Berlin 1961) 142.

131   Mark 12:1 says that Jesus began to speak in parables (plural), but
      only one parable follows. Matthew only says 'parable' at 21:33,
      and in this Butler finds confirmation of his view that Mark is excerpt-
      ing (*The Originality of St Matthew,* 88). But Matthew says 'parables'
      (plural), followed by one parable at 22:1!

132   There is some evidence that 'nor the Son' should be omitted in
      Matthew, and it is possible that the shorter reading is to be preferred.
      However, the words are well-documented in early representatives of
      the manuscript tradition, and their disappearance in other witnesses
      is probably to be explained as excision on theological grounds.

133   Goulder (*Midrash and Lection in Matthew,* 166) plausibly conjec-
      tures the influence of Paul on Matthew's eschatology.

134   *Ibid.* 83 - 5.

135   See Black, *An Aramaic Approach to the Gospels and Acts,* 223 - 5.

136   For difficulties about an Aramaic/Hebrew original for τὸ αἷμα μου
      τῆς διαθήκης see Gundry, *The Use of the Old Testament in St
      Matthew's Gospel with special reference to the Messianic Hope,* 58,
      n.2.

137   According to Streeter (*The Four Gospels,* 167) Luke at this point
      abandons blocks and uses two parallel sources.

138   Morton Smith, *Clement of Alexandria and a Secret Gospel of Mark.*

139   If this is correct, the problem of whether the Sanhedrin possessed
      capital jurisdiction, or whether they could condemn but not execute,
      or whether they needed the Governor's permission to meet formally,
      becomes less important. The point is that some members of the
      Sanhedrin wanted to get Jesus killed, but by the Romans. On the
      other issues I am inclined to think that the Sanhedrin did need the
      Governor's permission to meet (cf. P. Winter, *The Trial of Jesus*
      (Berlin 1961), esp. 16 - 19), and was able officially to recommend
      but not to carry out death sentences. But Jesus' enemies did not
      want an *official* recommendation. For the distinction between the
      right to sentence and the right to execute see most recently
      Catchpole, *The Trial of Jesus,* 254.

140   Such additions are designed to throw the blame on the Jews,

according to R. Bultmann (*Form Criticism* (New York 1962) 66).
Granted that the Evangelists may have wished to minimize possible
hostility from the Roman authorities, it does not follow that it was
unjust for them to attach varying degrees of blame to particular
members of the Jewish community - as is now often fashionably
suggested.

141   Cf. A. Guillaume, 'Mt xxvii, 46 in the Light of the Dead Sea Scroll
of Isaiah', *Pal. Exp. Quart.* (1951) 78 - 80.

142   For σαβαχθανι (from Aramaic) Codex Bezae reads ζαφθανει
(from Hebrew) in both Mark and Matthew.

143   W. R. Farmer (*The Last Twelve Verses of Mark* (Cambridge 1974))
has recently tried to argue that the question of the authenticity of
these verses is still open. I do not find his arguments at all convincing, though the matter cannot be discussed in detail here. Farmer's
view that Justin and Celsus provide evidence in his favour, i.e. for
inclusion, is unacceptable (p. 31). The evidence is much too uncertain. The first clear patristic evidence for inclusion is provided by
Irenaeus, and it is supported on the manuscript side by almost all
the Old Latin versions and by the Codex Bezae (D), as well as by
the 'Caesarean' witnessesΘ and 565, and, of course, a great variety
of other later MSS. On the other hand Sinaiticus and Vaticanus
omit the verses, and they are, strikingly, supported by the Codex
Bobiensis (it[k]) and by Sy[S] - to mention only the major evidence. It
seems that what can be deduced from this is that in the second century A.D. two traditions already existed, one omitting and one including the disputed verses. So that if the verses were added to a
defective Mark, this certainly happened early. But that they were
so added seems a likely deduction from the fact that it[k] and Sy[S] do
not, on this occasion, agree with D and the majority of the 'Western'
evidence. And this deduction seems, *pace* Farmer, to be supported
by an internal examination of the verses. In particular the shift of
subject and the fresh 'introduction' of Mary Magdalene in 16:9 are
not easily discounted. For a summary of other evidence see B. M.
Metzger, *A Textual Commentary on the Greek New Testament,* 3rd
edn. (London and New York 1971), 122 - 6. Farmer has been
effectively reviewed by J. N. Birdsall (*JTS* 26 (1975) 151 - 60).

144   Mary Magdalene is also omitted by Paul (I Cor. 15:5). In general
this passage of Paul may come from the source (or be in part the
source) of Luke 24:34ff.

145   *Pace* Streeter, *The Four Gospels* (343).

146   This source is hostile to 'the Jews', referred to thus at 28:15.

Phraseology of this kind, common in John, is unparalleled in
Matthew, though at 4:23 etc., as we have seen, we hear of *their*
synagogues' (cf. Mk 1:39); but that gives no real indication of date.
Cf. J. A. T. Robinson, 'The Destination and Purpose of John's
Gospel', *NTS* 6 (1960) 118.

147   Matthew is fuller at 3:7 - 12 (John the Baptist), 4:1 - 11 (Temptation),
4:12 - 17 (First Preaching), 4:23 (Preaching), 15:21 - 5 (Sections
of the account of the Syrophoenician), 23:1ff. (Against the Pharisees),
24:25ff. (the end of the Parousia), 26:50ff. (the Arrest).

148   Sanders, 'The Overlaps of Mark and Q and the Synoptic Problem',
462 and very explicitly in 'Priorités et dépendances dans la tradition
synoptique', 539.

149   *Ap.* Eus., *H.E.* 3.39.16.

150   R. H. Gundry, *The Use of the New Testament, passim.*

151   *Ibid.* 148.

152   *Ibid.* 179.

153   *Ibid.* 9.

154   It would not be implausible for Mark himself, as a bilingual author,
to follow the LXX in formal quotations, but to stick to his traditions
with their mixed textform in the Old Testament allusions.

155   Papias, *ap.* Eus., *H.E.* 3.39.6.

156   Ἑβραίδι διαλέκτῳ. The proposal of Kürzinger that Papias is concerned in this phrase with Matthew's style rather than his language
(thus ἡρμήνευσεν. refers to exposition) is attractive as a way out of
the difficulties Papias provides, but cannot be accepted. Irenaeus
(perhaps dependent on Papias) writes τῇ ἰδίᾳ αὐτῶν διαλέκτῳ.
(*adv. Haer.* 3.1, *ap.* Eus., *H.E.* 5.8.2, cf. *H.E.* 6.25.4 and note 163
below), which, with its definite article, points even more strongly to
language. (Origen also alludes to language, substituting γράμμασιν
for διαλέκτῳ (*Comm. on Matt., ap.* Eus., *H.E.* 5.23.4)). We should
also note that Irenaeus thinks that Matthew is earlier than Mark,
which our texts of Papias do not tell him. See p. 7.

157   Papias, *ap.* Eus., *H.E.* 3.39.15. For a good summary of the discussion
about the meaning of *logia,* and a clear statement that it must indeed mean 'Gospel' see D. Guthrie, *New Testament Introduction:
Gospels and Acts* (London 1965) 32 - 9.

158   *H.E.* 5.8.2 (*Adv. Haer.* 3.1).

159   For the Gospel of the Nazaraeans see *New Testament Apocrypha*
(ed. W. Schneemelcher, English version 1963) 117 - 53.

160   Eus. *Theophania* (Mai, *Nova Patr. Bibl.* IV, 1, 155).

161 Epiphanius thinks that the Hebrew 'Matthew' is our Matthew, but he obviously has not seen it (*Pan. Haer.* 29.2.4).

162 *Ap.* Eus., *H.E.* 3.39.1.

163 For 'handing down' cf. I Cor. 15:3($\pi\alpha\rho\acute{\epsilon}\delta\omega\kappa\alpha\ldots\delta$ $\kappa\alpha\grave{\iota}$ $\pi\alpha\rho\acute{\epsilon}\lambda\alpha\beta\omicron\nu$). For Peter witnessing see Acts 10:39. The Twelve devote themselves to prayer and the ministry ($\delta\iota\alpha\kappa\omicron\nu\acute{\iota}\alpha$) of the word in Acts 6:4; cf. Jn 21:24. Irenaeus has heard 'in tradition' that there are four Gospels (*ap. H.E.* 6.25.4).

164 This points strongly against Gundry's suggestion (The Use of the New Testament, 182 - 3) that Matthew's notes formed the basis for 'the bulk of the apostolic gospel tradition'.

165 For a good summary of the language situation in Palestine see Gundry *ibid.* 174 - 8. Some scholars have argued that at least Jesus' debates with the Pharisees may have been in Hebrew. Cf. the judicious discussion in Sanders, *The Tendencies of the Synoptic Tradition,* 203, and M. Black, 'The Recovery of the Language of Jesus', *NTS* 3 (1956 - 7) 305 - 13.

166 Cf. B. Gerhardsson, *Memory and Manuscript* (Uppsala 1961); H. Riesenfeld, *The Gospel Tradition and its Beginnings* (London 1957).

167 Patristic variants, however, may give us some pause in speaking of Jesus' words, as in the story of the Rich Young Man. Sometimes the gist of Jesus' words is enough (see below).

168 Cf. Jn 20:30: 'Now Jesus did many other things in the presence of the disciples which are not written in this book', and 21:25: 'But there are also many other things which Jesus did; were every one of them to be written, I suppose that the world itself could not contain the books that would be written'.

169 As Moule says (*The Birth of the New Testament,* 180): 'The Twelve were simply [*sic*] the initial authority for the Christian claims about Jesus'. (Cf. the title of the *Didache,* 'The Teaching of the Lord to the Gentiles through the Twelve Apostles'). Note Paul's claim to be an eyewitness of the Risen Lord (I Cor. 9:1): 'Have I not seen Jesus our Lord?'; cf. I Cor. 15:3ff.

170 There is too much loose talk about Matthew, Mark and Luke being theologians, for although this language is not entirely inaccurate, it can certainly be seen to be misleading, even when we compare the Synoptics with the Gospel of John.

171 Hence it is clearly important to Stendahl to *deny* apostolic authorship of the Gospels. Which is not to say that whoever wrote the Gospels may not have discussed his text with others.

172 *Ap.* Eus., *H.E.* 3.39.4. Cf. Irenaeus in a letter to Polycarp (*ap.* Eus.,
     H.E. 5.20.6 - 7 (ὑπομνηματιζόμενος αὐτὰ οὐκ ἐν χάρτῃ, ἀλλ᾽ἐν
     τῇ ἐμῇ καρδίᾳ). See also *Adv. Haer.* 4.32.1: 'et scripturas
     diligenter legerit apud eos qui in Ecclesia sunt presbyteri, apud
     quos est apostolica doctrina'; and Gerhardsson, *Memory and
     Manuscript,* 202 - 7, though Irenaeus' comments are not a reference
     to rabbinic-style teaching.

173 For the whole subject see H. Köster, *Synoptische Uberlieferung
     bei den apostolischen Vätern* (Berlin 1957, *TU* 65). Köster thinks
     that the influence of written Gospels on the Apostolic Fathers is
     very limited indeed. See his summary on Ignatius, p. 60; on I
     Clem., p. 23.

174 J. Smit Sibinga, 'Ignatius and Matthew', *Nov. Test.* 8 (1966)
     263 - 83. On p. 282 he argues that Ignatius may have known M
     in its pre-Matthaean form.

175 See p.58 and note 101.

176 See N. B. Stonehouse, *Origins of the Synoptic Gospels* (Grand
     Rapids, Mich. 1963) 16: He argues that the superscriptions on the
     Gospel manuscripts must go back to 140, if not to 125.

177 B. Gerhardsson, *Memory and Manuscript* (Uppsala 1961) 468,
     note 3.

178 R. H. Gundry, *The Use of the New Testament* 181 - 5.

179 For a good summary, see Klijn, *A Survey of the Researches into
     the Western Text of the Gospels and Acts, Part II,* 66 - 70.

180 *H.E.* 3.39.15.

181 This may mean the 'ex-interpreter' of Peter, and perhaps Irenaeus
     took it that way. But *pace* Lawlor and Oulton (*ad loc.*) this trans-
     lation is not necessary; indeed, it seems forced. If it were accepted,
     of course, it would date Mark after the death of Peter, as in Irenaeus
     - which would demand a slightly later date for Luke.

182 I take it that the *logia* here include both the words and the deeds of
     Jesus mentioned above. It is worth comparing the words of Eusebius
     (quoting Papias) with the words of 'Clement of Alexandria' as given
     in Morton Smith's newly discovered letter:

Papias	'Clement' (Plate I, fol. I, r, 1.16)
. . . ἔγραψε, οὐ	ἀνέγραψε τὰς πράξεις τοῦ κυρίου οὐ
μέντοι τάξει τὰ᾽ ὑπὸ τοῦ κυρίου	μέντοι πάσας ἐξαγγέλλων· οὐδὲ μὴν
ἢ λεχθέντα ἢ πραχθέντα	τὰς μυστικὰς ὑποσημαίνων ἀλλ᾽
. . . ὃς πρὸς τὰς χρείας	ἐκλεγόμενος ἃς χρησιμωτάτας ἐνόμισε
ἐποιεῖτο διδασκαλίας.	πρὸς αὔξησιν τῆς τῶν κατηχουμένων
	πίστεως.

Notes   129

183 *H.E.* 6.14.6. B. F. Westcott (*Introduction to the Study of the Gospels,* 7th edn. (London 1888) 193) may be right in thinking this is independent of Papias. After all, who would read Papias? Papias has no chronological information on Mark and Matthew. Irenaeus puts Matthew first, as we shall see, for Matthew is written 'while Peter and Paul were evangelizing in Rome'. According to Clement of Alexandria, those Gospels with genealogies were chronologically prior, and the priority of Matthew to Mark is also supported by Origen (*ap.* Eus., 6.25.4).

184 *Adv. Haer.* 3.1.2 (5.8.2). Some have tried to make ἔξοδος refer not to the death but to the 'departure' of Peter and Paul; this is misguided. We may note that in what *may* be the first patristic reference to Mark's Gospel (Justin, *Dial.* 106.3) the text is referred to as the 'Memoirs of Peter'. Memoirs of Apostles are mentioned also at 100.4, 104.1, 106.1 and 4.

185 Eus., *H.E.* 5.8.2 (Irenaeus), 6.14 (Clement), 6.25.4 (Origen).

186 *Op. cit.* 201.

INDEX

Abomination of Desolation 5, 81 - 2
Aland, K. 114
Aramaic Matthew 2, 20, 44, 60, 84, 87, 94, 96, 97, 98, 99, 100, 117, 124

Basic Gospel 14 - 16, 40, 58, 64, 79
Beatitudes 5, 26
Birdsall, J. N. 125
Black, M. 120, 124, 127
Brownlee, W. H. 122
Bultmann, R. 66, 122, 125
Burkill, T. A. 119, 122
Burney, C. F. 7, 115
Butler, C. 2, 4, 8, 11, 23, 57 - 8, 70, 74, 76, 82, 83, 108, 112, 113, 115, 116, 117, 118, 120, 121, 122, 123, 124

carelessness in Matthew 29, 60, 62, 77, 84
Catchpole, D. R. 115, 124
Chapman, J. 112
'Church' 6, 7, 69, 122
Crouzel, H. 73 - 4, 123
Cullmann, O. 122

date of Gospels 4, 6, 81, 97, 104, 106, 115, 119
Davies, W. D. 105, 115
divorce 72 - 5, 123
Dodd, C. H. 115
Dungan, D. L. 2, 113, 114

Farmer, W. R. 2, 4, 73, 75, 112, 113, 117, 125
Farrer, A. M. 8, 113, 115, 116
Finegan, J. 122
Fitzmyer, J. A. 113

Gaboury, A. 13, 17, 22, 30, 52, 54, 58, 63, 65, 101, 113, 117
Gerhardsson, B. 105, 127, 128
Goulder, M. D. 109 - 11, 114, 116, 119, 121, 123, 124

Griesbach, J. J. 2, 112
Guillaume, A. 125
Gundry, R. H. 95, 105, 116, 120, 122, 124, 126, 127, 128
Guthrie, D. 107, 126

Herod, Herodians 38, 63 - 4, 66, 119

Infancy Narratives 3, 110
interpolation 81, 105

Jameson, H. G. 112, 117
Jamnia 5, 6, 29, 115, 119
John the Baptist 17, 18, 19, 20, 21, 22, 63

Kilpatrick, G. D. 29, 115, 119
Klijn, A. F. J. 115, 125, 128
Köster, H. 128
Kundsin, K. 122

Léon-Dufour, X. 112
liturgical influence on Gospels 76, 85, 100, 102, 109
Lord's Prayer 26, 53

Matthew as notetaker 31, 105
Metzger, B. M. 125
Miracles added 68, 70, 89, 103
Mission to Jews, 7, 47, 48, 65
Morton Smith, R. 86, 94, 114, 124, 128
Moule, C. F. D. 105, 127

Neirynck, F. 112, 117

O'Callaghan, J. 114
order of pericopae 3, 11, 13, 14, 25, 26, 35, 46, 54, 59, 66, 93, 116

Papias 7, 96, 97, 98, 99, 103, 105, 106, 114, 129
parables 8, 41, 43 - 4, 49, 54